THE LITTLE GUIDE

Harrogate

The essential pocket-size guide

First edition

Contacts

THE LITTLE GUIDE

Harrogate
First Edition
Summer 2005

Published by Leeds Guide Ltd
30-34 Aire Street, Leeds LS1 4HT

General Enquiries	T: 0113 244 1000
	F: 0113 244 1002
	www.leedsguide.co.uk

Advertising 0113 244 1005
sales@leedsguide.co.uk

Design 0113 244 8484
design@leedsguide.co.uk

Editorial 0113 244 1007
editor@leedsguide.co.uk

Managing Director Bruce Hartley
Publishing Director Bill Graham
Editor-in-Chief Dan Jeffrey
Assistant to the MD Emma Parston

Editorial
Editor Abi Bliss
Contributors Naomi Attwood, Emily Boldison, Hazel Davis, Rory ffoulkes, Hannah Freegard, Kelly Gavaghan, Ben Jewitt, James Littlewood, Mollie McGuigan, Mark Sturdy, James Thwaite
Photography Victoria Baker, Sarah Healey, Elizia Volkmann
Cover Photo Zefa
Title Page Photo Paul Harris, courtesy of Harrogate International Centre

Studio
Blueprint Design 0113 244 8484
Senior Designer David Donaghy
Designers Laura Jukes, Evin Ozalp Sahin

Sales
Advertising Manager Ian Macdonald
Sales Executives Caroline Cooke, Kelly Gavaghan, Sarah Hallam, Richard Pope, Mark Walsh
Marketing & Distribution Executive Yasmin Poyntz
Printers Buxton Press
Distribution John Menzies UK Ltd

Contents

6 WELCOME

Just how much of Harrogate can you fit in your pocket? Read on and find out

20 HOT STUFF!
We sweat it out in luxury at the Turkish Baths

78 VILLAGE PEOPLE
5 reasons to leave town, if only for a day

92 VAN'S THE MAN
He'll be at this year's International Festival — will you?

112 PAD IT OUT
Harrogate property, from the modest to the millionaire-sized

Welcome to the first Little Guide to Harrogate

If you prefer fun to flowerbeds and style over scones*, then this book is for you.

Our pocket-sized guide gathers all that's best about the town: tastebud-tempting restaurants and bars; a varied nightlife with clubs, pubs, theatre and live music; shopping in stylish and individual boutiques and the top places to spend a lazy weekend. You'll find them all here, along with a few words from the locals on their favourite spots in town.

If you enjoy this *Little Guide*, then be sure to pick up your copy of *Plush*, Harrogate's essential monthly lifestyle title. And to find out what's happening each fortnight, look out for *Leeds Guide* magazine, with listings covering Harrogate, Leeds and York.

*Actually, we're all partial to the odd cream tea, so we've included a few places where you can find those, too. But don't tell anyone.

Shopping

From high-street to high-class, spending money in Harrogate is never difficult. Whether it's a completely new look (for your home, for yourself) or just that one vital item you seek, chances are you'll find it in a town centre where modern shopping centres brush shoulders with ornate arcades and where it's the shops that will sweep you off your feet, not the crowds.

Beach

Age Concern North Yorkshire
49 East Parade, Harrogate • 01423 502 253
From clothes, accessories and jewellery to bric-a-brac and bits, why not help some old people by rummaging here? What with Harrogate being so genteel and well-heeled and all, the items in their charity shops are often of a higher calibre than your everyday cast offs, so don't just walk past.

Arthritis Research Campaign
24 Beulah Street, Harrogate • 01423 562 785
Charity for arthritis sufferers; with a selection of secondhand gear: get your bargains here.

Austin Reed
21 Prospect Place, Harrogate • 01423 502 753

Beach
32 Beulah Street, Harrogate • 01423 524 600
This shop boasts a selection of branded ladies' and mens' wear. From fcuk to Criminal, Gas Clothing and, for the boys, Henleys and Duck & Cover, there is most everything here for lovers of jeans, T-shirts, tops and trainers with logos on 'em.

BHS
36-38 Cambridge Street, Harrogate • 01423 528 345

Bleyle
41 James Street, Harrogate • 01423 566 157

Burton
24 Cambridge Street, Harrogate • 01423 564 914

Cancer Research UK
7 Beulah Street, Harrogate • 01423 858 672

Country Casuals
37 James Street, Harrogate • 01423 562 499

Couture Candi
45 Parliament Street, Harrogate • 01423 875 887

Specialist ladies wear shop where the young and stylish can expect to pick up a wide range of labels and accessories. This welcome addition to Parliament Street has a great selection of trendy day and

Dorothy Perkins

eveningwear and plenty of space to try everything on in.

Dorothy Perkins
24 Cambridge Street, Harrogate • 01423 503 364

Dumblonde
2c Cheltenham Parade, Harrogate • 01423 507 990

Bleyle

G23

Lynx

A streety boutique stocking lotsa lotsa labels but with a laid-back, teenage-friendly atmosphere. Browse among the G SUS, Lou la la, Fornarina, Super Lovers shoes, jeans, T-shirts, ra-ra skirts and plenty more besides to the sound of indie beats.

East
18 James Street, Harrogate • 01423 508 529

Emma Somerset
24-26 James Street, Harrogate • 01423 502 109
Fancy ladies' wear, stockist of French Dressing.

Ernest Jones
34 James Street, Harrogate • 01423 817 020

Evans
2-4 James Street, Harrogate • 01423 562197

Footlites
42 Commercial Street, Harrogate • 01423 528 488
Specialising in dancewear, this quirky shop is your destination for all leotards, footless lights, leg warmers, pumps and tutus. Spandex, lycra and all in the most jazzy of colours, and service from the people who know their products.

G23 Harrogate
13 Cambridge Road, Harrogate • 01423 522 553
A must-see for branded and logo-based outfits for boys and girls over the spacious shop floor. Choose from Lee, Bench, Levis, Gold Digga, Firetrap and Miss Sixty for the girls to Jack Jones, Old Glory, Adidas and Firetrap for the gents.

GAP
2-6 James Street, Harrogate • 01423 528 938 ▶▶

dumblonde

street couture for men and women

ROUND FLOOR:

ASHION FOR SUGAR DOLLS
ND FUNKY DIVAS

FIRST FLOOR:

EDGY FASHION FOR MEN

SECOND FLOOR:

CREATIVE HAIR STYLING
FOR MEN AND WOMEN

RANDS INCLUDE:

FORNARINA
G-STAR RAW
RELIGION
BURN N VIOLET
RREGULAR CHOICE
LOOD AND GLITTER
RAFFIC PEOPLE
ND MANY MORE...

Where are we?

2c Cheltenham Parade
Harrogate
HG1 1DA

01423 507990
email: info@dumblonde.net

A Cut Above

Watch your step as you walk past Rhodes-Wood, else you might slip on Rory ffoulkes's drool

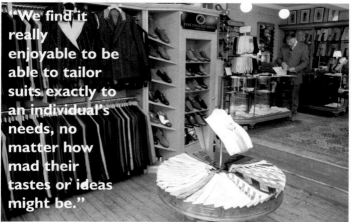

"We find it really enjoyable to be able to tailor suits exactly to an individual's needs, no matter how mad their tastes or ideas might be."

Rhodes-Wood are one of the very few tailors offering a bespoke, traditional service outside of London's Saville Row or Jermyn Street. Jeremy Beaumont and his then business partner, acquired the Harrogate shop eight years ago and Rhodes-Wood have fairly recently taken over a traditional tailor shop in Leeds, established in 1886:

"It was incredible to find the tailor working in the front of the shop, as they always used to, and we were absolutely adamant that we wanted to keep the tailor on. We just added our little touches, refurbished the shop and let him get on with it, working in the most traditional

manner", Beaumont says.

The British have forever worn suits, regardless of class, standing or financial position but, sadly, the fashion for wearing suits every day has disappeared over the last half-century:

"Dress standards have certainly dropped of late," remarks Beaumont, "most probably, I think, because of the negative effect that dress down day at work has had."

Such comments may, in the recent past, have been poo-poo-ed, dismissed as old-fashioned and stuffy. But bespoke tailoring is enjoying something of a revival, thanks mostly to the fact that young,

switched-on men have become rather bored with labels and are now looking to outdo their mates with individual, even eccentric, clothing.

Rhodes-Wood's clientele of course has its typical element: the country squire, the lawyer, the public schoolboy; but it also has a fresh group of customers made up of the young, trendy and slightly wacky. The beauty of bespoke tailoring is that you can have whatever you like made, so if you want to look like Willy Wonka, you can:

"We find it really enjoyable to be able to tailor suits exactly to an individual's needs, no matter how mad their tastes or ideas might be. We are also finding that young men, tired of the norm, are coming to us in order to have their designs made real."

A properly tailored suit can take up to eight to 12 weeks to make, so after the waiting is over, you had better make sure that you look after your suit in an appropriate manner.

"A suit's longevity is dependent both on its cloth and on rotation; if you switch suits every couple of days, you will find that your suits will last a great deal longer than if you keep wearing the same suit each week. Importantly, you should avoid dry cleaning where possible; it's a much better idea to simply sponge your suit, as the cloth will then not have to endure the damaging process of heavy dry cleaning".

Don't just go to Rhodes-Wood for your suits, though: all of their stock, apart from the Church's shoes, bear the unique Rhodes-Wood label and, let it be known that their shirts and ties are some of the very most beautiful that one will ever lay eyes upon. Anything that you pick up from Rhodes-Wood will turn your friends, if you have any, apple green.

56-58 Parliament Street, Harrogate, 01423 505 878

Local Focal

The word on Harrogate from the people who live there

❝ I've been here for about five years now. The open space is wonderful — you can quite easily get out to the countryside. For shopping it's got everything I need: Marks & Spencers, WHSmiths. In the centre the Old Bell Tavern is a nice place to go, and Beckwithshaw with the children.❞

Anna, "in my 30s", shop owner

▶▶ Goldsmiths
36 James Street, Harrogate • 01423 503 169

Hobbs
33 James Street, Harrogate • 01423 525 157

Hoopers
28-32 James Street, Harrogate • 01423 504 091

Rather fabulous looking emporium, a self-contained department store, with a bewildering array of fine designers, from the ubiquitous to the underground, stocking everything from Aquascutum to Fenn Wright & Manson to Wheels & Doll baby. Worth a gander for the imaginative window displays alone.

Jaeger
5 Cambridge Crescent, Harrogate • 01423 565 701

Jaeger Menswear
20 Prospect Place, James Street, Harrogate • 01423 528 818

John G
28 Station Parade, Harrogate • 01423 567 495

Gentleman's outfitters befitting of such a genteel location as Harrogate. Three piece suits, bow ties, ordinary ties, specialist shirts, possibly a cravat or two. Patronised by aficionados of waistcoats, canes, port and after dinner cigars the length and breadth of Yorkshire.

Littlewoods
29-31 Cambridge Street, Harrogate • 0870 163 4889

Lynx Menswear
12 West Park, Harrogate • 01423 521 420

Morgan Clare

Another haunt for those with a label fetish, (and in possession of a healthy sized croc wallet stuffed with plastic), as they pride themselves on their up-to-the-minute stock of Nicole Fahri and Replay to name but two. Fancy attire from an independent outlet that can satisfy your customer needs with an individual touch.

Marks and Spencer
36 Cambridge Street, Harrogate • 01423 526 221

McNally
27 Cheltenham Crescent, Harrogate • 01423 565 110
The luxurious interior of McNally houses racks of hand picked, feminine and directional pieces from underground designers. Jewellery, belts, bags, jeans and lots of lush evening wear from names such as Bruuns Bazaar and Lundgren & Windinge make this the shop for gals in the know.

Monsoon
20-22 James Street, Harrogate • 01423 501 469

Morgan Clare
Montpellier Gardens, Harrogate • 01423 565 709
If you're more interested in letting style come to you rather than hunting the racks for that special piece, Morgan Clare takes the hassle out of shopping with all the best

Dumblonde

designer labels such as Marc by Marc Jacobs, Mulberry and Joseph all under one roof, as well as Molton Brown products to pamper yourself when you get home.

Mothercare
Victoria Garden Shopping Centre, Station Parade, Harrogate • 01423 561 265

New Look
Victoria Shopping Centre, Harrogate • 01423 569 550

Next
Unit 8C Birstall Retail Park, Holden Ing Way, Birstall, Batley • 01924 421 350

NYC
Oxford Street, Harrogate

A good bet for both ladies and men's branded street wear, NYC has a particularly skater vibe about it. For jeans, baggy pants and trainers from which to hang your chunky chains look no further. From Carhartt to Paul Frank to Mooks to Zoo York to Drunk Munky with shoes by Duff, DC, Vans and the usual suspects.

Phase Eight
43 James Street, Harrogate • 01423 527 778

Porters Menswear
35 Oxford Street, Harrogate, North Yorkshire • 01423 522822

Upmarket menswear shop catering for discerning gentlemen and falling somewhere between the proliferation of branded goods and Lord of the Manor tailoring with a carefully chosen range of quality casual garb plus understated formal pieces. This shop would cater for confident dressers of all ages.

All you need to shop in Leeds
(except for your wallet)

The Leeds Guide Shopping Guide
Fully revised and expanded 4th edition
Out NOW!

Call 0113 244 1000 to order your copy

Sassy's

Rock One

33 Beulah Street, Harrogate • 01423 507 600

Everything for the hard labourin', outdoor workin' fellow here. From sturdy boots to florescent or padded gillets to overalls, anoraks, boiler suits and big gloves. Good for those who do manual work or else

Rose Velvet

those who dress up for fancy dress parties.

Rose Velvet

4 Montpellier Street, Harrogate • 01423 536 413

Girly girly whirly heaven in this boudoir style space, with all the flowers and textures and spangles and luxury a style-conscious resident or visitor to Harrogate could wish for. Rose Velvet has a reputation and press coverage that reflects its unique selection of merchandise, from lace parasols to classic evening pieces.

Sassy's

4 Oxford Street, Harrogate • 01423 567 389

A reasonably upmarket addition to Harrogate's undergarment retailers, Sassy's sells bits from different big brands, with a welcome emphasis on design, colour and femininity. Pink and yellow floral lace sets catch the eye on crossing the threshold.

Scholl

20 Oxford Street, Harrogate • 01423 504 831

Scholl, unlike most shoe shops, caters for both young and old with a selection of brightly coloured shoes and sandals available. With reasonably low prices and a handful of very helpful assistants, Scholl, although not the biggest of shops has a selection of footwear to suit all needs.

Scope
16 Parliament Street, Harrogate • 01423 566 524

Sunwin Department Store
5 Albert Street, Harrogate • 01423 523 731

This department store has a range of high street shops including Miss Selfridge, Topshop, Coast, Sisley, Mexx, Oasis, Faith and Fuse.

Taps & Tutus
24a Cheltenham Mount, Harrogate • 01423 530 777

Upmarket theatrical/performance wear, for river dancers and prima ballerinas, with a lot of sequins, stretch satin and improbably shiny shoes on display.

Tie Rack
Victoria Shopping Centre, Harrogate • 01423 527 877

Viyella
3 Prospect Crescent, Harrogate • 01423 566 815

WM Greensmith & Son
8 James Street, Harrogate • 01423 504 129

More upmarket men's tailoring for the well-heeled Harrogate chap. ▶▶

Scholl

All You Can Heat

Kelly Gavaghan experiences a day of delight at Harrogate's lovingly restored Turkish Baths

For the last month I have been charging around Harrogate and slaving away over my computer. I was in serious need of some good old-fashioned R&R. So when Lucy Dale, Manager of the Turkish Baths invited me try out the experience, plus a couple of treatments to boot, who was I to look a gift horse in the mouth?

Last year the Turkish Baths was restored to all its former glory and it is absolutely exquisite. Everything now is how it would have been in Victorian times. There are some wonderful, quirky features that were uncovered by the workman such as the glass brick tiled

ceiling/floors that now allows a lot more light in and the changing and toilet cubicles which have had the gloss paint stripped off to reveal beautiful rich, oak. The stencilled paintwork, particularly in the Relaxation Room has been copied from old black and white photos. To get the perfect colour match, the workmen stripped back the layers to the original paint stencilling and have recreated it beautifully.

Lucy advised me to just bring along my personal toiletries as fresh, soft, fluffy white towels are provided. After changing into my costume, Christine, who runs the historic guide tours for the Baths, took me from room to room explaining their purpose and the process.

First of all you need to take a warm shower to remove any body creams and oils before entering the Plunge Pool. This where you have to brace yourself as it is cold with a capital C. On entering it's best to take shallow breaths and swim a couple of laps to keep the circulation moving.

After this I entered the Turkish Steam Room. I much prefer the steam to a sauna's dry heat. Being much gentler it enables you stay in longer and really give your skin a chance to breath and sweat out all the unwanted toxins. This room is particularly good for asthmatics and people with sinus problems as the eucalyptus oil combined with the steam really cleans you out.

After showering I started to work my way up through the three inter-connecting hot room chambers. I started in the Trepidarium (warm) where you can relax on wooden lounge beds and either just lie back and clear your mind or read. There are also fresh water facilities in the corner of the room. You are advised to continually drink water so as not to dehydrate. I took another plunge in the cold pool after this and moved onto Calidarium (hot), plunged again then finished in the Laconium (the hottest: 70°C!).

In the last two chambers there are towels laid out on the marble seating surfaces so as not to burn yourself. It really *is* hot — but it is lovely. When I was walking around with Christine at the beginning the heat in these chambers had felt slightly uncomfortable, even with my bathing suit on. However, after you start the process incorporating the cold plunge pool, the temperature in the chambers feels right, nice and comfortable. I could have kept going all day. For the first time in quite a while I felt calm, tranquil and peaceful and it's a feeling that enveloped

▶▶

me immediately on entering the Baths.

It is advised that you spend at least two hours at the Turkish Baths to reap the full benefits of the experience and you must allow yourself time to cool down and allow your blood pressure to return to normal by resting in the beautiful Frigidaruium (relaxation room). Otherwise you will leave feeling light-headed and woozy. At the end of this thoroughly wonderful experience I had a gorgeous feeling of warmth, cosiness and well-being. I'll definitely be visiting the Baths again.

Turkish Baths and Health Spa, Royal Baths, Parliament Street, Harrogate, 01423 556 746, www.harrogate.gov.uk

For Peat's Sake

Nowdays a session at the Baths is treat to look forward to; but if it had involved some of the 'therapies' from 100 years ago, chances are you wouldn't be quite so eager...

Then: Intestinal Lavage Treatment

Colonic irrigation may be a favourite of modern celebs (not to mention Gillian McKeith from 'You Are What You Eat'), but our ancestors were also fond of 'lavage' (things always sound more sophisticated in French, see?). If all that grand Edwardian dining had left you feeling a bit off-colour, then the two-way continuous irrigation system would soon sort you out.

Now: Platinum Detox

Similar to electrolysis experiments you may remember from school science lessons, this involves your feet being placed in a foot spa whilst a current is conducted through the water. Proponents claim that the treatment draws toxins out through your feet; although it may come as a relief to realise that the resulting yucky brown water colour is actually due to corrosion of the electric coil and not some inner evil being released. Either way, it's more relaxing than having your insides sluiced.

Then: Peat Baths

Unfortunately for the Edwardians, they were yet to discover Lindow Man who lay buried in a Cheshire bog for 2000 years. If they had seen his complexion, perhaps they would have thought twice before making patients sit immersed in a bath of the Yorkshire Moors' finest. Rheumatism and sciatica were among the ailments this was thought to benefit.

Now: Montecelli Mud/Remineralising Wrap

Today's beauty treatments may still involve getting messy, but at least there's no danger of finding a group of ramblers trekking across you mid-treatment. This is much classier stuff, being a creamy sea mud enriched with Italian thermal waters and essential oils. A foreign holiday for your skin, no less!

AB

Accessories

&eve

3a John Street, Harrogate • 01423 705 652
Feminine and reasonably priced high heels, kitten heels, strappy sandals boots and bags for party girls and style mavens on a budget.

Antonio Fattorini

10 Parliament Street, Harrogate • 01423 502 440
The Fattorinis have a long history, dating all the way back to 1827, when the company was first founded. There is a wide selection of jewellery and watches, along with helpful staff who know their stuff.

Azendi

15 Station Square, Harrogate • 01423 566 366
A beautiful range of jewellery designed in-house and by partners in Italy and Germany. With over 90% exclusive to Azendi you can be assured to find an original piece.

Bijoux

2 Oxford Street, Harrogate • 01423 560 323
Hippy and rave-style jewellery, clothing and home furnishings par excellence. From inexpensive watches to tie-dye tops to record bags, body jewels to spangly scarves, cushions and slogan T-shirts.

Bradley's

16 Princes Street, Harrogate • 01423 709907
6 Prospect Crescent, Harrogate • 01423 525 500
The Bradleys have been selling classic pieces of jewellery for over 30 years. Everything from diamond rings to pearl sets

&eve

is available here, along with friendly staff that know their stuff.

Clarks

13-15 Market Place, Harrogate • 01423 569 975

Cruise

Posh shoes, jewels, hats bags and boots for ladies and gentlemen over two floors.
44-46 James Street, Harrogate • 01423 568 170

Duttons For Buttons

7 Opera House Buildings, Oxford Street, Harrogate • 01423 502 092
Not strictly a clothes or accessories shop, nevertheless any girl worth her fashion salt recognises the importance of haberdashery, and has a good browsing location in mind. All manner of buttons, sequins, feathers and trims for your delectation. All you will need is a needle and thread and a touch of imagination. ▶▶

At Her Leisure
Kelly Gavaghan relaxes at Nidd Hall Hotel

Nidd Hall Hotel has a lot to offer, including the well equipped leisure club set within the beautiful grounds of this majestic hotel. There are a wide range of club facilities, such as the indoor pool, spa and plunge pool, steam room, sauna, solarium, as well as outdoor tennis courts, bowls and archery.

There are also a number of health and beauty treatments available in the suite, including back, neck and shoulder massage using Swedish massage techniques and aromatic facials using Decleor products to leave you with a sense of wellbeing and glowing skin.

After treatments, you have the luxury of being able to go through to the pool and spa. There are floor to ceiling arched windows all along one side of the 20-metre pool allowing in lots of natural light and a view of the plants and beds outside. It's very clean, light and airy, offering an environment where people can enjoy a full range of leisure activities at their own pace, however relaxed that might be.

Nidd, Harrogate, 01423 771 598

Jones Bootmaker
5 James Street, Harrogate • 01423 858 102

Vivo Jewellery
4 Commercial Street, Harrogate • 01423563636

Smart looking boutique showcasing a fine array of funky contemporary silverware, from pendants and cuffs to bracelets and bangles and from sleek designs to flower motifs and semi-precious stones in desirable, modern settings.

Health & Beauty

Harrogate Health And Beauty
25 Ripon Road, Harrogate • 01423 563 108

For fifteen years this salon has been providing a range of procedures from collagen boosters to permanent make-up along with the regular range of treatments such as waxing, facials and tinting. The staff regularly take training courses and go to conferences on beauty therapy so you are guaranteed to be in good hands.

Nidd Hall Hotel
Nidd, Harrogate • 01423 771 598

A hotel with a difference, Nidd Hall is just as well known for its relaxing beauty treatments as the hotel itself. The facilities include a heated swimming pool with spa pool and also a steam room and sauna to banish all stressful thoughts and detox the skin. The facials and massages on offer will help you have a truly relaxing stay.

Sheila Henry Hair and Beauty
29 Park Parade, Harrogate • 01423 561178

This upmarket salon provides every

Azendi

treatment you can imagine for both men and women. Tanning, facials, haircuts, collagen — you name it they've got it and all in a beautiful relaxed setting with friendly staff who know their stuff.

The Clarins Studio
Hoopers, 7- 11 Princes Street, Harrogate • 01423 564 514

With over 50 years of expertise under their belt, you can be guaranteed of a special experience at Clarins. They offer a range of treatments including aromatherapy and make-up master classes along with massage and facials for men.

U Beauty
4 Union Street, Harrogate • 01423 567 900

This stylish salon does a huge array of treatments to suit your needs, for men and women including ear piercing and massage.

The Japanese Shop

There is also the option to create your own day package, choosing what suits you best.

Westrow

81 Station Parade, Harrogate • 01423 522 666

This stylish salon is worth the prices: they have won countless awards and take hairdressing very seriously. There are a range of products to purchase along with top class, professional advice.

Home & Leisure

Art Apartment

The Mill, Green Dragon Yard, off Castlegate, Knaresborough • 01423 867 606

A three-storey selling gallery of art and design for interiors and gardens.

Blooms of Harrogate

22 High Street Starbeck, Harrogate • 01423 880 024

Blooms stock a massive selection of cut flowers as well as some potted plants and shrubs. They are available for weddings and deliveries, so that's valentines sorted.

Books For All

23a Commercial Street, Harrogate • 01423 561 982

Here you can find a selection of second hand and rare books to suit all your needs. It's easy enough to spend hours here, searching the shelves for those one-off classics

Chalon

The Piazza Unit, Station Parade, Harrogate • 01423 523 182

This shop defines luxury. Grand four-poster beds, freestanding kitchens and beautiful crafted dining room furniture. They offer an interior design service, which caters for all your homely needs, including designing pieces of furniture to your specification. Like I said, luxury.

Exit Lifestyle Interiors

34 Parliament Street, Harrogate • 01423 858111

Contemporary accessories, furniture and lighting especially for those looking for something quirky or different. A great range of gifts with a specialist gift service also available for weddings etc.

Formative Fun

9 Beulah Street, Harrogate • 01423 501 157

In a similar vein to the Early learning Centre, Formative Fun stocks toys that are fun and educational. In fact, some of them look downright intriguing. Fancy starting an ant farm, growing crystals or caring for some Sea Monkeys? Then this is the place to visit.

Four Seasons

63-65 Cold Bath Rd, Harrogate • 0808 144 0808

Florists.

Gascoigne Gallery

Royal Parade, Harrogate • 01423 525 000

Selling gallery with a preference for landscape and figurative work, mainly from local or locally related artists.

Gone Potty

1a Westminster Arcade, Parliament St, Harrogate • 01423 705 666

This quaint shop sells ceramics from the UK, Spain and Estonia. There is a small selection of artwork, clocks and gifts. Worth the visit alone is the magical toy display in the window.

Chalon

Henshaws Arts & Crafts Centre
50 Bond End, Knaresborough • 01423 541 888
Excellent selection of weaving, pottery, paper-making, knitting, jewellery, horticulture, woodwork, music and drama and 3-dimensional work (including felting and mosaic).

Magpie Greetings
4 Westminster Arcade, Harrogate • 01423 505 803
Thinking of sending a gift? Then this is the place for you. There is everything you could think of here including witty cards, wrapping paper and kooky gifts such as jumping beans and flying saucer balloons.

March Hare Craft Gallery
1 Ripon Small Shops, Duck Hill, Ripon • 01765 608 833
Affordable handmade art and craft in a welcoming and friendly atmosphere minutes away from Ripon Cathedral and nestled away in a Victorian style arcade.

Mercer Art Gallery
Swan Road, Harrogate • 01423 556 188
The gallery has a small shop with post cards, books, catalogues and prints.

Original Arts
5 Station Bridge, Harrogate • 01423 567 600

This selling gallery specialises in ceramics, glass and jewellery as well as paintings from regional artists.

Ottakar's

15 James St, Harrogate • 01423 531 953

Although a chain, this bookshop strives to create a sense of individualism in all its branches. They support book awards such as The Orange Prize and The British Book Awards and keep customers informed with bestseller lists and book clubs.

Out and About

18 Bower Rd, Harrogate • 01423 561 592

Stockists of a wide range of camping and outdoor equipment. The prices are good too, so you will have money left over to buy some batteries for that torch.

Past Times

18 Prospect Place, Harrogate • 01423 705 252

Specialists in gifts with a 'ye olde' feel to them; here you can pick up water features, jewellery and books. It may not be everyone's idea of tasteful but there are some beautiful pieces hidden away among the nymphs and gnomes.

Ponden Mill

2 Nidderdale House, Cambridge Rd, Harrogate • 01423 566 469

This store may lack the stylish displays of others but it's not to be sniffed at. There are a stack of bargains here and although cheap, there is good quality linens, cushions and furnishings here.

Richard Axe Books

12 Cheltenham Crescent, Harrogate • 01423 561 867

A great selection of both rare and secondhand books can be found here,

from all genres. It's a wonderful place lose yourself in.

Rocking Horse

2c Cheltenham Parade, Harrogate • 01423 566 718

Giant inflatable banana anyone? When you see the diverse range of toys on this stall, you'll quickly realise it's filled with 'whatever I can get my hands on' rather than carefully chosen from a stock catalogue, unless of course, the owner has amazingly eclectic taste. And that's a good thing. This isn't the kind of place you come when you have a specific item in mind; it's a fun place to spend a couple of pounds. Hula hoop? Dumper truck? Airfix kit anyone?

Smallbones of Devizes

10 Princes Street, Harrogate • 01423 529 222

Smallbones sells beautiful kitchen, bedroom and bathroom units. Whether it's their latest kitchen collection made of walnut and silver or gothic doors for your bedroom, you can choose a design, which suits you.

Special Days

131 Otley Rd, Harrogate
Florists.

The Aga Shop

2 Grosvenor Buildings, Crescent Road, Harrogate • 01423 505 494

So, you've got the green wellies, the house in the country and the Labrador. All you need now is for Harrogate's Aga Shop to weave their real-fuel magic and hey presto: tonight Matthew, I'm a member of the landed gentry. They'll even come visit your studio flat for free to assess the suitability.

Art Apartment

The Gift Consultancy

47 Parliament Street, Harrogate • 01423 508 515

Bespoke wedding gift service. The shop retains unique and individual gifts whilst the showroom, situated on the first floor, provides comfortable surroundings in which couples can plan their wedding lists. The online service (www.thegift consultancy.co.uk) means people can even select items from home. The whole range of traditional gifts (china, glassware, linen) is provided, as well as more unusual gifts such as weekend breaks, furniture and art.

The Japanese Shop

1 Westminster Arcade, Parliament Street, Harrogate • 01423 529 850

This shop sells beautiful and colourful kimonos for all shapes and sizes. There are also Hiroshige prints and jewellery by Damascene.

Toy Box

184 Kings Road, Harrogate • 01423 701 709

Set away from the main shopping area, this small shop reminds you of the ones that you used to see on every high street. Expect a cheerful welcome and as much or little help as you need while you browse the shelves. Corgi model cars, wooden spinning tops and pocket money toys — it'll take you back a bit!

Toymaster

47-49 James Street, Harrogate • 01423 564 335

Now this is a great idea. Take locally owned specialist toy shops, bring them all together, and what have you got? The perfect combination of friendly service and buying power. This means you can expect to be helped by someone who really knows about toys and can bring their own personality to the shop. And you don't have to pay through the nose for it. Brilliant.

Up and Running

16 Station Parade, Harrogate • 01423 562 345

Family-run store who are experts at fitting trainers, with a comprehensive selection from the affordable to top of the range.

Woods of Harrogate

65-67 Station Parade, Harrogate • 01423 530 111

Directed by interior designer William Woods, there are a huge variety of luxury goods for bedroom, bathroom and kitchen. They also offer an interior design service, with a team of craftspeople making curtains and furnishings to your specification.

Yeoman's

39 Oxford St, Harrogate • 01423 569 111

Everything you need for camping is available here: stoves, tents and mats. You name it, they've got it. If you can't find the shop, look for the two huge flags waving outside. Not hard to miss.

Food & Drink

Three courses please, waiter! To start, we'll have some of Harrogate's finest restaurants, from long-established favourites to new and exciting dining flavours. Next we'll hit the town's cafes and bars for a drink and a bite — with everything from cream teas to live music on the menu. And to finish, what could be better than a serving of the best pubs around? Harrogate suits every palette.

Restaurants

Albert's

2 Albert Street, Harrogate • 01423 568 446

Ali Raj Tandoori

7 Cheltenham Crescent, Harrogate • 01423 521 627 • Open Sun-Thu 6pm-12am; Fri-Sat 6pm-1am. Vegetarian friendly.

Attic

62a Union Street, Harrogate • 01423 524 400 • Open Mon-Sat 12-2pm, 6.30-10pm. With a self-professed aim to stimulate its customers' senses in relaxed, unhurried surroundings, The Attic has an almost holistic approach to the dining experience. The menu is diverse and interesting, and offers dishes that change seasonally, though prices are what you might expect from this stylishly designed two-floor venue; this is the price you pay to be seen in one of a new breed of fashionable Harrogate restaurants. The Attic also offers a cheaper earlybird menu Monday to Thursday (including lunchtimes).

B.e.d

24 Kings Road, Harrogate • 01423 568 600 • Open Mon-Sat 10am-11pm. Thoughtful, cosy restaurant that doesn't take itself too seriously as far as décor and menu blurb is concerned (signs ask cheekily "who will you spend the night in B.e.d with?" and you'll find 'Me mom's chocolate cake with curly wurly ice cream' amongst the desserts), but is serious as they come when it comes to food. The menu is full of good honest fare — haddock pie, pan fried salmon fillet, mixed grill — prepared unfussily. The result is a vast spread of well put-together, homely and very tasty food. The earlybird menu — £25 for two courses and a bottle of house wine for two people — is spectacularly good value.

B.e.d

Bower's Bistro

Bengal Spice

21 Cheltenham Crescent, Harrogate •
01423 502 610 • Open Sun-Thu 6pm-
12pm; Fri-Sat 6pm-1am. Vegetarian friendly.
The great British tradition of falling out of
the pub into the curry house dictates that
sometimes you'll need a place to go that's
both simple, and great value. Bengal Spice
is perfectly situated and most importantly it
opens late. Using only fresh ingredients,
and sporting a fully licensed bar that's
stocked with Kingfisher, Cobra, and Lal
Toofan lagers, customers can expect a high
standard of all the famous curry dishes and
some high quality house specialities. Great
value complete dishes for larger parties can

also be ordered at twenty-four hours
notice.

Biscaya Bay

11-13 Mount Parade, Harrogate • 01423
500 089 • Open Mon-Sat 6-10pm.

Bower's Bistro

31 Cheltenham Crescent, Harrogate, North
Yorkshire • 01423 565 806 • Open Tue-Sat
12pm-2pm, 6pm-12am. Vegetarian friendly.
Offering a la carte starters and mains (with
some vegetarian options) at reasonable
prices, this centrally-located venue has
proved to be very popular with locals and
visitors, its elegant and simple décor
creating a cosy Parisian-style atmosphere.

Brio Ristorante

44 Commercial Street, Harrogate • 01423 529 933 • Open Mon-Sat 12-2pm, 6-10.30pm. Vegetarian friendly.

Brio Hornbeam Park

Unit J1, Hornbeam Park Drive, Harrogate • 01423 870 005

When Gianni Bernardi sold his old restaurant the loss of one of Harrogate's best-loved town centre Italians was widely mourned. But luckily the force behind Gianni's bounced back with three new restaurants. Alongside its popular counterparts in Leeds, Harrogate's Brio offers endless Mediterranean energy and verve that filters down from the chefs and

waiting staff to the food on your plate. Able to cope with intimate meals for two or larger parties, Brio is a memorable experience, their menu is mouth-watering true Italian cuisine without the pizzas, and daily specials are also available.

Casa Romana

23 Cheltenham Crescent, Harrogate • 01423 568 568 • Open Mon-Sun 12-2.30pm, 5pm-late. Vegetarian friendly.

Cattlemans Association

17 Cheltenham Crescent, Harrogate • 01423 561 456 • Open Mon-Sun 5pm-10pm. Vegetarian friendly.

Trends come and go but the Cattleman's Association endures. As one more

Cinnamon Room

interesting option on the restaurant-heavy Cheltenham Crescent area of the town, it offers genuine homegrown Texan fare for cowboys, conference delegates, and anyone with a big big appetite. With its dark wood Saloon style interior, replete with Yankee flag and bulls horn décor, the gut-busting steaks and burgers mean you should allow yourself a few hours to be fed and watered and a few spare notches on your belt for afterwards.

Cedar Court Hotel

Queen Building, Park Parade, Off Knaresborough Road, Harrogate • 01423 858 585

As Harrogate's oldest hotel, Cedar Court has been servicing visitors to the town since 1671. The menu aims to incorporate traditional Yorkshire cooking with modern European cuisine, using local produce wherever possible. So expect to see Nidderdale trout, Yorkshire blue and all sorts of local goodies on the menu. Desserts are equally worth getting excited about, with hearty traditional puds like apple and Black Sheep ale pie existing alongside more contemporary desserts.

Cheaug Won

7 Cheltenham Parade, Harrogate • 01423 538 538 • Open Mon-Sun 12-3pm, 5-11pm. Vegetarian friendly.

With the cheeky look of a fast food outlet and the type of modern city-centre atmosphere that many of the town's restaurants don't possess, this noodle bar has a cartoon look and feel. Cheung Won is popular with younger diners and is a great place for a quick noodlefest, or a buffet meal and beers. Located on Cheltenham Crescent, and adjacent to the theatre and

Cutlers on the Stray

bus station, this is worth a visit if you're in a hurry, or just want to fill up on tasty Chinese fare.

Chez la Vie Restaurant
92 Station Parade, Harrogate • 01423 568 018

Chimney Pots Bistro
Grants Hotel, 3-13 Swan Road, Harrogate • 01423 560 666 • Open Mon-Sun 6-9.30pm. Vegetarian friendly.

Cinnamon Room
34 Oxford Street, Harrogate • 01423 505 600
First floor restaurant with glass walls allowing you to bathe in the jealous looks of the hungry masses below. Fortunately, the food more than meets the standards set by the surroundings. This is top class Indian

fare — the tandoori trout is strongly recommended. Impressive location, excellent food and all for an absolute steal — once tried you'll find it difficult to eat a curry anywhere else without being massively disappointed.

Courts Wine Bar & Restaurant
1 Crown Place, Harrogate • 01423 536 336 • Open Mon-Sat 11am-11pm; Sun 12-10.30pm. Vegetarian friendly.
With an interior that is reassuringly cosy, like being invited into someone's living room, Courts is relaxation for Harrogate's over 25s (a strict door policy ensures it). Sophisticatedly dark, it's perfect for the candlelit romantic dinner for two. If you like it a little louder, they also put on theme nights - recent ones have included a Rat Pack Las Vegas night - and a live pianist.

Cutlers on the Stray

19 West Park, Harrogate • 01423 524 471 • Open Mon-Sat 12-2.30pm, 6-11pm; Sun 12pm-3pm, 6pm-10pm. Vegetarian friendly. With its informal design, open fires, clean wooden candlelit tables and wrought-iron chairs, Cutlers is a perfect place to idle away a long lunch, bar snack or evening meal. Located on the site of one of Harrogate's oldest hostelries, and near to the old tollgate entrance to the town, Cutlers' 19 bedrooms have views across the town's impressive Stray. Special offers on food and wine are also available for lunchtime diners and drinkers.

Damn Yankee

4 Station Parade, Harrogate • 01423 561 424 • Open Mon-Thu 12-2pm, 5-10pm; Fri 12-2pm, 5-10.30pm; Sat 12-10.30pm; Sun 12-10pm. Vegetarian friendly.

The Damn Yankee requests that you have an American-sized appetite to deal with its home-made burgers, Mexican dishes, steaks, salads and sandwiches. An old favourite with Harrogate diners, Damn Yankee is now in its third decade. With the look of a 19th century American outpost, expect to witness the staff racing up and down with pitchers of frothy lager and spectacular desserts. The famous Scooby Snack is worth a sample if you can face a double burger with double bacon, cheese, onion and chilli.

Dr B's Restaurant

13-15 Knaresborough Road, Harrogate • 01423 884 819 • Open Restaurant Mon-Fri 12-2pm; Cafe Mon-Fri 9am-3.30pm. Vegetarian friendly.

Hotel Du Vin

Drum & Monkey

5 Montpellier Gardens, Harrogate • 01423 502 650 • Open Mon-Sat 12-3.30pm, 6.30-10.15pm. Vegetarian friendly.

Still ahead of the competition and situated near some intriguing antique shops, the Drum and Monkey is at the heart of old Harrogate. Newcomers be warned, from the exterior it does appear to be distinctly eccentric, residing as it does in the shell of an old pub and sporting a non-PC stuffed monkey in military uniform in the window. However, with its cosy upstairs dining area and good service it's highly recommended. Don't expect bargain prices, and do book early if you want to land a table.

Dusty Miller

Low-Laith, Summerbridge, Harrogate • 01423 780 837

Dynasty Chinese Restaurant

12 Kings Road, Harrogate • 01423 858 667 • Open Mon-Sun 12pm-2pm, 6pm-9.30pm

Est Est Est

16 Cheltenham Crescent, Harrogate • 01423 566 453 • Vegetarian friendly.

General Tarleton

Boroughbridge Road, Ferrensby • 01423 340 284 • Food served Mon-Sun 12-2.15pm, 6-9.15pm. Vegetarian friendly.

Graveleys

8-10 Cheltenham Parade, Harrogate • 01423 507 093 • Open Sun-Thu 11.30am-2.30pm, 4.30-9pm; Fri-Sat 11.30am-10pm.

Gravelys continues to expand and develop, and manages to combine the homely charm of its fish and chips background with an ambitious and wide-ranging fresh seafood menu that includes lobster.

All The Fun Of The Fare

Farrah's Food Hall is one of Harrogate's mouthwatering institutions. Victoria Baker salutes a shop with famously good taste

Established in 1840, Farrah's original business was in the now famous Harrogate Toffee, with its inimitable butterscotch and barley sugar flavour. It's still their most prominent product and is made in Harrogate to this day along with ginger biscuits, creamy caramels and other goodies.

A few years ago Farrah's launched their own label products adding local handmade cake bakers, Bainbridges, to their range and expanded their girth further with a deli counter stocking local meats and cheeses, spicy salamis and freshly ground coffee. Opposite the counter you can find fine wines, quality cooking staples such as olive oils or ready made sauces for fresh pasta

should you want something more instant.

What assaults your senses as you enter the shop though is the rich smell of chocolate. Adults and children alike peer into the elongated curved glass counter agonizing over the layers of creamy chocolate truffles, bitter ganaches and coconut ices stacked like bars of gold bullion. Even if you're too young to remember the traditional sweetshop, Farrah's Olde English Sweet Jars conjure up nostalgic childhood memories and transports you to the good old days of long summers, skipping ropes and eeking out your pocket money for just a few more sherbet lemons.

So the next time you're about to embark on the weekly supermarket shop and enter the strip-lighted world of clattering trolleys and customer announcements, remember the cut glass chandeliers, sturdy oak fittings, gold embossed packaging and the mouth watering rows of jams, preserves and honey lining the walls at Farrah's. Just the thought of this should spur you to cut up your Nectar card and make a dash to Montpellier Parade to savour food heaven.

29 Montpellier Parade, Harrogate, 01423 525 266, www.farrahs.com

Le D2

▶▶ A number of overhead-heated tables are positioned in front of the restaurant under a permanent wood and glass canopy. You can expect great service in this fun family-run business.

Harrogate Brasserie
28-30 Cheltenham Parade, Harrogate • 01423 505 041 • Open Mon-Sun 6pm-10pm. Vegetarian friendly.

With its chessboard floor, cosy bar and dining rooms, the Brasserie is the perfect place for an intimate dinner or a special gathering of friends. The graceful interior design recalls an older, less fast-moving era with a good use of dark woods, red walls, and black and white photography. Time spent here is rewarding and guests will find that all the bedrooms are individually decorated. The Brasserie also offers regular live Jazz evenings in its bar and members of the general public are always welcome.

Horoscope

1 Cheltenham Crescent, Harrogate • 01423 508 144 • Open Sun-Wed 5.30-11pm; Thu-Sat 11am-1.45pm, 5.30-11pm.

Serving Peking, Cantonese, and Szechaun cuisine this is an old favourite with Harrogate diners. With its simple red and white interior, and discreet blinds over wide windows, Horoscope is neat, pristine, and polite. There's a small bar area where you can wait for your table to be prepared while you witness authentic and beautifully prepared food come sizzling from the kitchen. With its convenient town centre location, this is a popular and consistently enjoyable place to eat.

Hotel Du Vin

Prospect Place, Harrogate • 01423 856 800 • Open Mon-Sun 12pm-1.45pm, 6.30pm-9.45pm. Vegetarian friendly.

The highly regarded Hotel Du Vin is a friendly affair with its impressive stone bar, low lighting and the wise absence of mood music that establishes a calming atmosphere. The incredible phone-book-sized wine list includes wines from every corner of the globe, whilst the food fully justifies the prices.

Jinnah Restaurant

34 Cheltenham Parade, Harrogate • 01423 563 333

Joe Rigatoni

3 Ripon Road, Harrogate • 01423 500 071 • Open Mon-Sun 6pm-late. Vegetarian friendly.

If you like your Italian food served with style this is the place for you. A pasta and pizza restaurant that's set apart from the town centre bustle, with pleasant views towards

Le Petit Bistro

the Majestic Hotel. Joe Rigatonis is hugely popular with families and group parties. What it sometimes lacks in atmosphere it makes up for with delicious food and drink. The service is excellent, so expect to be waited on hand and foot from the second you arrive.

Kinara

19 Cheltenham Crescent, Harrogate • 01423 530 715

La Tasca

1 John Street, Harrogate • 01423 566 333 • Open Mon-Sat 11am-12am; Sun 12-10.30pm. Vegetarian friendly.

Another inhabitant of John Street, this Spanish tapas bar and restaurant welcomes drinkers and diners, and is the best place to eat on this popular bar-filled side street. La Tasca offers overhead-heated tables that should allow paella fuelled merriment to

continue long into the occasionally not-so-balmy British summer nights.

La Terrazza

28 Swan Road, Harrogate • 01423 508 111 • Open Mon-Sat 6.30-10pm. Vegetarian friendly.

Le D2

7 Bower Road, Harrogate • 01423 502 700 • Open Tue-Sat 12pm-2pm, and 6pm-9.30pm. Gluten-free dishes, Vegetarian friendly.

A joint venture between the previous owners of Ville Toots, Le D2 aims to offer 'high quality French cuisine accompanied with excellent service.' The conservatory interior gives off an ambience of French country chic, and the atmosphere is generally relaxed and friendly with a mixed clientele. The menu offers typical French fare, including a superb 'Coti de Boeuf' (serves two), a 2lb rib of Yorkshire beef with all the trimmings, for diners who fancy more than just a petit morceau. The two course lunch deal, priced at a modest £6.95, also makes Le D2 a popular place to stop and recharge after a morning shopping.

Le Jardin

7 Montpellier Parade, Harrogate • 01423 507 323 • Open Lunch: Mon-Fri 11am-2.30pm; Sat 10am-5pm. Candle-lit bistro: Wed-Fri from 6pm

Le Petit Bistro

33 Montellier Parade, Harrogate • 01423 569691

Loch Fyne Restaurant

Town Centre Square, Cheltenham Parade, Harrogate • 01423 533 070 • Open Mon-Thu 9.30am-10pm, Fri-Sat 9.30am-

10.30pm, Sun 10am-10pm. Vegetarian friendly.

Beautifully designed, Loch Fyne's mature and modern interior is candle-lit, wooden walled and includes a covered balcony that is ideal for summer lunches. The menu offers a wide-range of fresh seafood at good prices: main courses range from the excellent fish pie to lobster. Ideal for a chilled evening out with friends.

Lords Restaurant

Like many of the town's enduring restaurants Lords is quite hard to locate. Nestled close to the Montpellier quarter, its simple décor and predominantly British menu (with an emphasis on local produce) continues to be highly popular. Lords is quite small and always popular, so at weekends it's worth ringing ahead for a table.

8 Montpellier Street, Harrogate • 01423 508 762 • Open Tue-Sat 12-2.30pm, 6.30-10pm; Sun 12-8pm. Vegetarian friendly.

Luigi's Restaurant

1a Valley Drive, Harrogate • 01423 560 311

Loch Fyne

Lords

McDonalds

5-6 Nidderdale House, 14-16 Cambridge Road, Harrogate • 01423 523 544

Mill 67 Bistro

Skipton Road, Felliscliffe, Harrogate • 01423 779 909

Nidd Hall Hotel

Nidd, Harrogate • 01423 771 598 • Open Wed-Sun 6.30-9.30pm. Sun: 12-2. Gluten-free dishes, Vegetarian friendly.

This grade II listed hotel, which plays host to holidaying couples of a more mature variety, contains within it the Oak Room, an á la carte restaurant open to all where fine dining precedes a nice bit of dancing.

Olley's Pizzeria

Bridgehouse Gate, Pateley Bridge, Harrogate • 01423 712 200

Orchid/Studley Hotel

28 Swan Road, Harrogate • 01423 560 425 • Open Mon-Sat 12-2pm, 7-10pm (Sat excludes lunch).

Orchid restaurant occupies the ground floor of the Studley Hotel, which makes it harder to spot. It's an unusual juxtaposition — the hotel embodies the usual Harrogate values, with old stone walls and a prim and proper garden, whilst the restaurant space is a very modern mix of laminate flooring, white walls and sleek furniture. A huge range of choice on the menu offers a blend of East Asian cuisine, although the food is unexpectedly hit and miss. Some dishes, like the Vietnamese sea bass, are glorious feats of flavour combination; others, like the vegetable dumplings, are a non-event.

Is your restaurant on the menu?

To advertise in the next edition call 0113 244 1000

The Courtyard

Phoenix Cantonese Restaurant

73 Station Parade, Harrogate • 01423 563 045 • Open Tue-Sun 12-1.30pm, 5.30-10.30pm. Vegetarian friendly.

Serving high-quality Cantonese food, Phoenix has a look that makes you think of 60s James Bond films. Step beyond the imposing red and white exterior and you'll find walls decorated with enormous Oriental fans and paintings, and a tropical

fish tank next to the bar. The friendly waistcoated waiting staff are always attentive and the menu is varied and tasty, offering some good value set meals, including a vegetarian option.

Pinocchios Restaurant

Empire Buildings, Cheltenham Parade, Harrogate • 01423 560 611 • Open Mon-Fri 12-2pm, 5-10pm; Sat 12-10pm; Sun 12.30-9.30pm. Vegetarian friendly.

Pinocchio's is situated in a building that was originally built as the Empire Theatre and played host to the likes of Sarah Bernhardt and Fats Waller. Pinocchio's has been one of the town's most popular Italian restaurants since its opening in the 1970s. A family business with a warm atmosphere, it remains a regular haunt for patrons of the nearby theatre. Don't be surprised to see candlelit cakes and hear the strains of 'Happy Birthday', sung heartily by the always good-natured waiting staff, it's a much-loved tradition here, and has made Pinocchio's particularly popular with kids.

Pizza Express
2 Albert Street, Harrogate • 01423 531 041

Pizza Hut
19-21 Parliament Street, Harrogate • 01423 524 396

Quantro
A seductive little place that exudes luxury and quality. And naturally, for a restaurant that specialises in French cuisine, the food is generally very flamboyant.
3 Royal Parade, Harrogate • 01423 503 034

Raj Put
11 Cheltenham Parade, Harrogate • 01423 562 113 • Open Mon-Sun 5-12pm. Vegetarian friendly.
Raj Put's menu is mouth-watering. Dishes include the ever-popular chicken korma and bhunas as well as an imaginative selection of non-meat dishes like chana cheese masala, a cheese and chickpea dish, and badal jan, an exotic aubergine dish. If you don't want to wait for a table the best time to go is early in the evening, though if you have to wait for a while there is a small bar serving great Lal Toofan lager.

Reinaldo's Tapas Bar
18 Kings Road, Harrogate • 01423 563 680

Rudding Park Hotel
Rudding Park, Follifoot, Harrogate • 01423 871 350 • Open Mon-Sun, 12.30-2pm, 7.30-9.30pm. Gluten-free dishes, Vegetarian friendly.

Salsa Posada
4 Mayfield Grove, Harrogate • 01423 565 151 • Open Sun-Thu 5-10pm; Fri-Sat 5-10.30pm. Vegetarian friendly.
Having been in business for over 15 years Salsa Posada can probably lay claim to be one of the first Mexican restaurants in the UK. With a proven and highly popular menu this tiny slice of Mexico has remained unchanged for many years and still offers hot and crisp burritos, chimichangas, and fajitas. Prices aren't cheap but the food is

Wild Ginger

Drum & Monkey

a lunchtime retreat from town centre shopping.

Shahnaz Indian Restaurant
24 Station Parade, Harrogate • 01423 527 532

Smiths Arms
Church Row, Beckwithshaw, Harrogate • 01423 504 871

Starbeck Tandoori
67h High Street, Harrogate • 01423 888 414

Surma Tandoori
1a Oxford Street, Harrogate • 01423 520 539

Tannin Level
5 Raglan Street, Harrogate • 01423 560 595 • Open Mon-Sat 12-2pm, 5.30-10pm. Vegetarian friendly.

One of Harrogate's best known and most popular restaurants The Tannin Level offers an extensive à la carte menu, fixed menu, lunchtime and early bird menu and an impressive wine list. Diners normally descend into the Princes Square basement dining area but there are a limited amount of marble-topped outside tables available with fine views of Harrogate's elegant Princes Square.

TGI Friday
John Street, Harrogate • 01423 509 357

Clean, shiny new branch of the US chain, much like any other outpost of the TGI empire only smaller. The look is 50s burger bar chic mixed with random pop culture grab bag (unaccountably, there's a *Ghostbusters* skateboard on the wall), whilst the food is hearty if rather expensive burger fare and the range of cocktails is huge and silly.

always of a very high quality. With its wooden floors and tables, Mexican art and sombreros, this is a vibrant place to eat and drink.

Sasso
8-10 Princes Square, Harrogate • 01423 508 838 • Open Mon-Sat: 12pm-2pm, and 6.30pm-10pm.

One of the most elegant and simple Italian restaurants in town, but don't expect to find pizza here, this is a strictly antipasto and pasta affair. Situated just below ground level with views out onto the attractive Princes Square, Sasso is small with an old-fashioned look and feel. Its tiled floor, wooden tables, clean linen, and sparkling glasses make it a perfect spot for an intimate evening meal or

Thai Elephant

15 Cheltenham Parade, Harrogate • 01423 530 099

Located directly above Yoko's Teppanyaki, this medium-sized restaurant has been popular for some years. Serving authentic Thai cuisine in generous amounts with a pleasant homely interior and good-natured staff, this is a reliable and fun place to eat. Prepare to happily while away the time studying the menu, and sipping an oriental beer or two.

The Courtyard

1 Montpellier Mews, Harrogate • 01423 530 708 • Open Mon-Sat 12-2.30pm, 6.30-9.30pm. Vegetarian friendly.

Montpellier Mews is a town centre collection of antique shops, cafés, and restaurants. The Courtyard Restaurant is a real find if you want to get away from the familiar. This independently run restaurant offers an à la carte menu with lunchtime and evening set menus and specials. As its name suggests it also has a cosy and secluded cobblestone courtyard with a small number of tables for alfresco dining.

The Italian Connection

51-55 Cold Bath Road, Harrogate • 01423 564 160 • Open Tue-Sat 10am-4pm; Fri-Sat 7pm-late. Vegetarian friendly.

During the day you can drop in to The Italian Connection for an espresso and a dolcelatte sandwich, or just to buy some freshly made lasagne or ciabatta. But on Friday and Saturday evenings its small restaurant area is transformed into an authentic Italian-style eatery. Patrons can expect to enjoy wonderful fresh pasta dishes and good wine in this informal and friendly family-run business.

Local Focal
The word on Harrogate from the people who live there

❝ I've lived in Harrogate six years now. It's very nice, picturesque. For shopping it's alright, but I still tend to go back to Leeds quite a lot. There's no shortage of places to eat or drink: there are some very nice restaurants. The Rajput is very good.❞

Barvinder, 31, assistant gallery manager

Bar Med

The Pavillions Restaurant
21-22 West Park, Harrogate • 01423 505 871

The Thai Royal
4-5 Baines House, Station Parade, Harrogate • 01423 522 222

The Willow Restaurant
8-10 Park Road, Pateley Bridge, Harrogate • 01423 711 689

The Yorke Arms Hotel
Ramsgill-in-Nidderdale, Pateley Bridge • 01423 755 243

Villu Toots
Franklin Mount, Harrogate • 01423 705 805 • Open Sun-Fri Lunch; Mon-Sun dinner. Vegetarian friendly.

Wild Ginger
5 Station Parade, Harrogate • 01423 566 122 • Open Tue-fri 10am-3pm;Sat 11am-7pm. Gluten-free dishes, Vegetarian friendly.

A cosy bistro hiding behind shelves of TVP packets in a health food shop, Wild Ginger's vegetarian fare is much more easy-going than the packets of dried goods and herbal treatment posters would have you believe. Serving snack-y burgers, jackets and sandwiches during the day, in the evening the candlelight and yellow walls give it a cosier, intimate feel. Starters include potato wedges with fresh-tasting and distinctive dips such as broad bean and freshmint and sundried tomatoes, butterbean and lime, whilst mains include meat-free versions of haggis and sausages guaranteed to keep the most unwilling vegetarian happy. Desserts — such as crunchy-topped peach and apple crumble — have a nostalgic, homemade quality.

William & Victoria Restaurant
6 Cold Bath Road, Harrogate • 01423 521 510

A secluded bistro-style restaurant with the a wine bar upstairs, William and Victoria provides the best of traditional English food, via popular dishes like roast pork with apple sauce and vegetables. Main courses are plentiful with deserts following the same delicious trend, and the atmosphere is relaxed and comfortable. The wine list is impressive.

Yaks Mongolian Barbeque
Orient Townhouse, 51 Valley Drive, Harrogate • 01423 565 818

Yoko's Teppanyaki Japanese Restaurant
Azelea Court Hotel, 56-58 Kings Road, Harrogate • 01423 817 945

One of Harrogate's best-kept secrets, Yoko Tepanyaki Japanese restaurant is part of the Azalea Court Hotel situated on Kings Road opposite the famous International Conference Centre. With a full menu of delicacies (the lobster and scallops are

particularly good) and a set menu of five-course house specials it's an ideal place for a romantic evening meal or lunchtime socialising.

Yoko's Teppanyaki

15 Cheltenham Parade, Harrogate • 01423 502888 • Open Mon-Sun:12pm-2pm and 6pm-11pm. Gluten-free dishes, Vegetarian friendly.

The most recent of chef Yoko Banks stylish restaurants, Yoko's Teppanyaki is small, but perfectly formed. Tucked away on Cheltenham Parade, the gentle outdoor water feature and minimalist décor will appeal to any stressed soul.

Zizzi

Town Centre House, Cheltenham Parade, Harrogate • 01423 507 391 • Open Mon-Sun 12-11pm.

A pizza and pasta restaurant opened as part of the well-known Ask chain, this is a new addition to Harrogate's long list of Mediterranean dining spots. With its authentic wood-fired pizza ovens, and a spacious interior that combines relaxing creams and browns and neat and clean surfaces, it is ideal as a place to fill up before a night on the town, or relax and watch the people wander up and down Cheltenham Parade.

Cafes & Bars

Bar Med

Royal Baths, Parliament Street, Harrogate • 01423 701 012

Having transformed the Royal Baths into a gaudy bauble, Bar Med was the first of a new complex of brand bars that now make the lower end of Parliament Street the

Cafe Rouge

Betty's Cafe Tearooms

busiest and boldest part of town. With its vast complex of well-designed interior rooms, that include a dancefloor, a endless bar, and quieter dining areas serving Mediterranean food, this is not so much a bar as a mini cruise ship. If you require lager-fuelled intensity and a high-energy evening this is worth a look.

Betty's Cafe Tearooms

1 Parliament Street, Harrogate • 01423 502 746

The Harrods of tearooms. With cakes that give you a sugar rush just by looking at them, eating in Betty's is an expensive treat. Paradise for kids, and more work for their dentist. Be prepared to queue before they can stuff themselves with treats from the formidable Fat Rascal menu (with matching crockery, no less) while you refuel with one of the potent speciality coffees.

Blues Bar

4 Montpellier Parade, Harrogate • 01423 566 881 • Open Mon-Sat 10am-11pm; Sun 10am-10.30pm. Vegetarian friendly.

Now in its third decade this much-loved Harrogate institution has always been the keystone of alternative drinking in the town. A friendly independently owned bar it has a 'Cheers'-like cast of regulars propping up the bar, but also manages to appeal to new generations who prefer their bars to be less corporate. With a genuine whiff of bohemia about it, the Blues hosts quality live music on Saturdays and Sundays, and some weeknights. Special note should also be given to its selection of lagers from around the world, and the collection of Kevin

Dining Out 05/06

BRADFORD HARROGATE LEEDS YORK

The essential guide to
eating out across the region

Out Now Call 0113 244 1000 to order your copy

Restaurants • Cafes • Bars • Sandwich Shops • Dining In

THE **LEEDS** GUIDE

Local Focal

The word on Harrogate from the people who live there

❝ Nice surroundings, loads of fields. For drinking I like Wetherspoons and the Rat & Parrot. It's getting better for shopping — Sunwin House is pretty good, and TopShop and Miss Selfridge.❞

Carla, 19, nursery nurse

Reynolds black and white prints that adorn the interior walls.

Cafe Rouge

21-27 Beulah Street, Harrogate • 01423 500 043 • Open Mon-Sat 10am-11pm; Sun 10am-10.30pm. Vegetarian friendly.

Adjacent to Deflifrance is Harrogate's thoughtfully designed Café Rouge. Attractive outdoor seating stretches along the length of the café's canopied frontage, allowing patrons to soak up the sun while sampling the set menu and daily specials. The waiting staff are typically friendly and attentive, and the food and drink is ideal for a quick snack or hours of pseudo-Parisian lingering.

Carriages

89 High Street, Knaresborough • 01423 867 041 • Open Mon-Thu 5-11pm Fri-Sat12-11pm Sun 12-10.30pm. Gluten-free dishes, Vegetarian friendly.

Probably the best place to eat out in Knaresborough, Carriages' home-cooked tapas menu is the perfect accompaniment to an afternoon spent under an umbrella in the bar's fun-sized suntrap garden. With views down towards the railway station and viaduct and down to the Nidd it's an impressive and relaxing place to sit out and enjoy great food and drink. If the tapas doesn't grab you then something from the à la carte menu or wine cellar is certain to do the trick.

Christies Wine Bar

20 Kings Road, Harrogate • 01423 507 971

Delifrance

31 Beulah Street, Harrogate • 01423 520 262

Revolution

Delifrance is situated on Beulah Street, which is one of Harrogate's many pedestrianised town centre thoroughfares. It has established itself as a busy stop-off point for freshly prepared French-style light meals and drinks. Its enthusiastic staff are welcoming, and the venue's street-side seating area is a popular choice for morning, lunchtime, and afternoon patrons.

'Gate

51 Parliament Street, Harrogate • 01423 502 759 • Open Mon-Thu 12pm-11pm; Fri-Sat 12pm-12am; Sun 12pm-10.30pm.

After a recent rebranding, the bar formerly known as brb thankfully still excels in being relaxed and friendly. A great place to be when it comes alive in the evenings and laid-back during the daytime, expect to find

convivial staff serving great pizzas, wraps, and salads. The basic design is soft chrome, knotty wooden tables, fairy lights, and comfy leather sofas and chairs. The ever-changing displays by modern young artists make regular visits a pleasure, and newcomers should take a peek at the enormous black leather bed that lies waiting in the upstairs bar.

Ginnel Cafe

The Ginnel, Harrogate • 01423 530 022

Hales Bar

1 Crescent Road, Harrogate • 01423 725 570 • Open Mon-Sun 4pm-11pm. Vegetarian friendly.

Situated in clear sight of the Royal Pump Room Museum Hales's has become part of the fabric of this part of town. Retaining its

So!

centuries old charm Harrogate's oldest pub boasts two bars with different personalities. Turning left at the entrance the small snug bar has a traditional taproom feel, while the grander lounge bar retains its 19th century high ceilings, curved leather seats, and original gas fittings on the bar. Popular lunchtime pub food and real ales are served seven days a week.

Hedleys Wine & Food Bar

5-7 Montpellier Parade, Harrogate • 01423 562 468

Currently celebrating its 25th anniversary, Hedley's restaurant has recently been refurbished. This unassuming and relaxed wine bar offers superb views of The Stray and West Park. Stripped pine tables and soft lighting create the ambience, and the food is excellent home-cooked rustic fare. The popular early bird menu is also well worth consideration for pre-theatre or cinema dining.

HG1

John Street, Harrogate • 01423 526 841 • Open Mon-Sat 11am-1am; Sun 11am-11pm. Vegetarian friendly.

Situated at the back of the historic Imperial Hotel, with an entrance on the pedestrianised and bar heavy John Street, expect to see a comfortable and sophisticated design in chocolate browns, maroon and silver metalwork. Though not entirely original this is a civilised place with an atmosphere that mirrors the congenial hotel. HG1 also serves lunchtime and early evening food from an interesting á la carte menu.

Lounge

7-11 Princes Street, Harrogate • 01423 705 234 • Open Mon-Thu 11am-11pm; Fri-Sat 11am-1am; Sun 12-10.30pm.

With its uplit ornate ceiling and long wooden bar this is a roomy venue that more than earns the right to its laid-back name. Candlelit tables, and wide curvaceous leather sofas hugging a long curtained wall are some of its main features. Serving lunchtime food the atmosphere transforms from chic and civilised during the day, to a livelier pre-club crescendo by closing time.

Lounge Inn Focus

The Small Shops, Duck Hill, Ripon • 01765 698 235

Merchant Stores

3 John Street, Harrogate • 01423 536 651 • Open Mon-Sun 11am-11pm; Food served Mon-Sun 11am-4pm. Vegetarian friendly.

Though lacking in the refinement of its near neighbours, Merchant Stores remains a popular place to eat and drink. Daytimes are laid-back, and on sunny days seating spills out on to the pedestrianised John Street. Much of its drawing power is in its location, and the chance to observe the designer label-obsessed people of Harrogate waltz past with a fresh haul of shopping bags. With two large screens and fruit machines most pastimes are catered for.

Milans

47 Oxford Street, Harrogate • 01423 536 606

Located just a stone's throw from bustling Parliament Street, Milans is one of the oldest buildings in Harrogate. This rustic coffee shop with a twist provides the hungry shoppers and residents of Harrogate with a great selection of snacks and homemade cake. And it's not just the food that's deserving of your attention. The building was once owned by James Franklin who famously bought all of Harrogate for nine thousand pounds.

Slug & lettuce

Native State

Monteys Rock Cafe

Corn Exchange Buildings, The Ginnel, Montpellier Parade, Harrogate • 01423 526 652

Although it's only been around since the late 90s, Montey's has quickly become an institution in both Harrogate and Knaresborough. In the past couple of years it's been given a facelift, losing the blues image of old in favour of a more general "rock down the ages" sort of slant. Cocktails, shooters, a heated outdoor area and Sunday night acoustic sessions complete the picture.

Montpellier Bar

14 Montpellier Parade, Harrogate • 01423 817 300

The Montpellier used to look slightly down at heel among neighbouring antique shops and squeaky clean cafes, but since a re-design a couple of years ago what was a pleasant but unremarkable pub has come alive. Sporting bright-coloured interior

upholstery and wall-encased fish tanks that allow aquatic creatures to peer out at you while you drink, it's now more Club 18-30 than Saga. A great place to sit out when the sun bathes this verdant part of Montpellier Gardens, you'll also find live music is available throughout the week, favouring laid-back acoustic duos rather than full-on bands.

Olivers Cafe-Bar

Victoria Shopping Centre, Harrogate • 01423 520 926

Pitcher & Piano

5-6 John Street, Harrogate • 01423 565 628 • Open Mon-Sun 11am-11pm.

Located on John Street, close to town and the Stray it's a popular choice for worn-out shoppers or frazzled workers. Often very busy on Friday and Saturday bouncers patrol the doors and queues form down the alleyway outside. The décor is simple and sophisticated and the atmosphere is

relaxed. The menu offers light snacks, platters to share, small courses and main courses from a range styles.

Prego

2 John Street, Harrogate • 01423 705 557
This sleek and shiny sandwich and coffee bar is a relative newcomer to John Street. The food is fresh and of a high quality, and the simple blue, orange and silver design is refreshing and cool. In the summer months seating spills out on to the pedestrian-only street allowing you to relax as busy shoppers and tourists flow past your eyes.

R Bar

2a Albert Street, Harrogate
R Bar is a tiny and friendly cellar bar that serves chilled beers to chilled customers. The bar also boasts a great old fashioned sit down Pac Man machine, a cosy alcove, full sized traffic lights on the bar that tell you when it's closing time, and a snack dispenser that resembles a Rubik's puzzle. If that isn't enough to tempt you downstairs

then you'll also find a friendly welcome and an eclectic selection of music.

Rat and Parrot

11 Prospect Place, Harrogate • 01423 564 976
Housed in an imposing five-storey Georgian building, overlooking West Park, and The Stray, The Rat and Parrot is impossible to ignore. Outdoor seating is front-facing with great views of those picture postcard Harrogate scenes and with plenty of potential exposure to the sun — ideal for relaxed drinking and dining.

Revolution

Unit 3, Royal Baths, Montpellier Gardens, Harrogate • 01423 858 815 • Open Mon-Sun 11.30am-12am, full menu served till 9pm. Evening menu served till 12am. Vegetarian friendly.
Vodka is the new black, you know. Which is good news for Revolution because it's got lots of vodka (around 40 flavours), it's (relatively) new and it's (predominantly) black. Good for them. The vibe is

Olivers Cafe-Bar

Old Bell Tavern

resolutely night-time orientated, with late opening hours, quality DJs every night and stylish, subdued décor. Comfy, lively and always packed.

Slug & Lettuce

13a-13b Montpellier Parade, Harrogate • 01423 508 444 • Open Mon-Sat 11am-11pm, Sun 12-10.30pm. Vegetarian friendly. Located in the old Akrill Newspaper building, the Slug and Lettuce is bright, and airy throughout, and offers street-front

seating with beautiful views of Harrogate's Montpellier Gardens and The Stray. A recently opened patio garden is situated at the rear, which is sheltered and peaceful. The set menu is combined with ever-changing specials and a good selection of wines, beers, and soft drinks.

So!

1 Silver Street, Knaresborough • 01423 863 202 • Open Mon-Sat 11am-11pm, Sun ▶

Drink And Be Merry

The local pub gems where you'll encounter a far from hostel reception

Old Bell Tavern

Hales Bar

Hales is the oldest pub in Harrogate, a Grade II listed building that's been there since the 17th century. As such, it's fitting that even the lighting is gas-powered and dates back to the Victorian era. And if that wasn't enough to make it unique, it's also the only gay-friendly pub in the village.
1 Crescent Road, 01423 725 570

Old Bell Tavern

Bill Clinton's been here you know. According to the plaque on the wall, he visited on the 8th of June 2001 and dined on the homemade Steak and Ale Pie. Good taste, that Bill. The Old Bell

opened in 1999 but you wouldn't know it — there's very little about the décor that suggests the place has been altered at all since the 1950s. Authentic vintage mahogany fixtures and fittings abound, as do an impeccable range of real ales alongside a variety of German and Belgian beers, an extensive wine list and some high-quality homecooked food.
6 Royal Parade, 01423 507 930

Coach & Horses

The primary outlet for Starbeck's acclaimed Daleside brewery, the Coach & Horses is a friendly and relaxed atmosphere in which to enjoy some of Yorkshire's finest real ales. Also some

excellent traditional pub meals, superb wines and the largest selection of single malt whisky this side of Scotland.
16 West Park, 01423 568 371

Montey's

Montey's is that rare thing, a music-orientated town centre boozer that dares to be different by eschewing the usual chart stuff, instead providing a background of masterfully chosen nostalgic rawk and live acoustic talent. A fine place to while away an afternoon or evening, especially with the genius happy hour. Five shots for a fiver? Get in!
The Ginnel, 01423 526 652

Smiths Arms

Out in the wilds of Beckwithshaw, the Smiths Arms is a traditional old country pub that's well worth visiting. Once a blacksmiths, it's now a cosy eating house with a couple of open fires which are very welcoming in the cold wintry weather that you've probably had to brave to get there. No loud music, no telly, just well-prepared old-skool pub grub washed down with quality wines or real ales.
Church Row, Beckwithshaw, 01423 504 871
MS

Hales Bar

▶▶ *11am-10.30pm. Food served Mon-Sun 12-9.30pm.*

So!, as you'd imagine from the name, is a rare nod to modernity in the Knaresborough boozing scene - it's big, it's light, it's chilled, it's got clever branding and it serves good food and decent wine. Don't worry though — it still lives up to its location by having three real ales on tap at any given time.

Stalls Bar

Cheltenham Parade, Harrogate

Likeable tavern attached to the rear-end of Harrogate Theatre, vaguely resembling a crypt hewn from rock, but with arty quotes and Phill Jupitus adverts on the walls. As well as obviously being the watering hole of choice for passing thesps, this sporadically doubles as a lively gig venue.

Subway

14 Beulah Street, Harrogate • 01423 817 755

The Loft Tea Room

Green Dragon Yard, Knaresborough • 01423 860 949

Set in Green Dragon Yard among the art galleries and holistic therapy centres, the 1930s-themed Loft tearoom spills out onto the cobbles bringing its pre-war England theme into the sunshine. Ideal for a big slice of cake and a strong cup of tea this is a chance to get away from the bustle of this busy market town.

Pubs

Black Swan

17 Devonshire Place, Harrogate • 01423 563 234

Blind Jack's

8a Market Square, Knaresborough • 01423 869 148

Named after the famous local wonky road-maker and pretty much the definitive

Pitcher & Piano

Knaresborough hostelry, Blind Jacks is a cosy, friendly, 'grown up' sort of place whose nods to the modern world start and end with the existence of a non-smoking room. This is good. No music, impeccable range of ales, dark wood panelling and floorboards, warm friendly atmosphere, three flavours of crisps. Marvellous.

Blue Bell Inn
Moor Lane, Arkendale, Knaresborough • 01423 340 222

Boars Head Hotel
Ripley Castle Estate, Harrogate • 01423 771 888

Chequers Inn & Restaurant
Bishop Thornton, Harrogate • 01423 770 173

Claro Beagle
Coppice Gate, Ripon Road, Harrogate • 01423 569 974

A true community pub with a very lively sports following. It comprises three separate areas, each with a unique style. The first is a straightforward bar with an excellent range of drinks. Secondly, there's the sports area, with pool tables and big screen Sky TV. Lastly there's a quieter lounge and relaxation area, well-suited to families.

Coach and Horses
16 West Park, Harrogate • 01423 568 371
Situated on the corner of Tower Street and West Park, this is one of the town's favourite traditional pubs. Always welcoming, it offers homemade lunchtime food ranging from chef's specials to a choice of baguettes and toasties. Specialising in real locally brewed beers, you can expect to be offered anything from

Flares

Black Sheep Bitter, Old Legover, Greengrass Old Rogue Ale, Daleside Bitter, to the legendary Monkey Wrench. The interior is all old mirrors and smoky charm, and is perfect for whiling away the hours while the world speeds by outside.

Devonshire Arms
10 Devonshire Place, Harrogate • 01423 503 892

Eddisons
North Eastern Chambers, 1 Station Square, Harrogate • 01423 725 740

Flares
46 - 48 Parliament Street, Harrogate • 01423 566 576
Fun, cheap and cheesy as they come, Flares is the kitsch '70s theme bar taken to its logical extreme. Silly music, afro wigs, floral shirts, bright lights and glitz. And if that's not enough, there's the 2am bar at weekends and vast quantities of cheapish booze. If the sound of that appeals, you're home and dry. And if it doesn't? Start drinking at 5pm after you finish work on Friday. By the time

Food & Drink

you stagger down Parliament Street five hours later, you'll find that garish red and purple sign is suddenly strangely enticing...

Harrogate Arms
Crag Lane, Harlow Carr, Harrogate • 01423 502 434

Jack's
Station Square, Harrogate
Essentially a venue transplantation of former legendary Harrogate haunt Jack & Danny's. Only without Danny. Themed Americana/rock bar with posters of everyone from Aerosmith to 'Zeppelin, plus the obligatory Route 66 signs and knackered Gibsons on the wall. Serves good cheap drinks, has regular live music, and is always buzzing. Well worth a visit.

Knox Arms
Knox Lane, Harrogate • 01423 525 284
Located in Bilton, a quiet suburb on the fringe of Harrogate, The Knox Arms has a strong local reputation for reasonably priced home-cooked food, and a great beer garden for summer afternoons. They offer a large comfortable lounge bar, with a quiz night and live

entertainment. The pub also houses a games room, with pool, darts, dominoes and a jukebox.

Montpellier Bar
14 Montpellier Parade, Harrogate • 01423 817 300
The Montpellier is a bright, airy pub with colourful sofas and some extraordinarily fat goldfish in a tank set into the wall. Having undergone a couple of major refurbishments in recent years, this focal point of Harrogate's exclusive Montpellier Quarter is a treat to visit.

Muckles
11 West Park, Harrogate • 01423 504 463
With its motto "we turn every customer into a regular" this is one of a trio of pleasant real ale pubs on and around the main West Park thoroughfare. After a brief spell as an Irish theme pub Muckles has now returned to something close to its original character — a sports pub boasting five TVs and a big screen. Serving lunchtime pub fare, catering for small parties and hosting quiz nights, this is a decent place to enjoy a relaxing drink with friends. And should you stay a little too long, they also offer B&B rooms.

Nag's Head
13-15 Parliament Street, Harrogate • 01423 525 390
Known for a long while as the Hogshead, a change of hands last year resulted in a crafty reworking of the sign outside and little else. It's still a biggish, pleasant town centre establishment with light, woody décor and a range of drinks that pushes it towards the upper scale of such

'Gate

things. And? Music video on the telly, pool tables upstairs. That's about it really.

Native State

18-20 Parliament Street, Harrogate, North Yorkshire • 01423 538 701

This used to be Lloyds, so the low-key but modern brown interior, no-nonsense selection of drinks and fair dinkum Wetherspoons-esque food on offer should come as no surprise. Other points of note include the weekly Sunday house night FKUC and lots of cocktails.

Nelson Inn

Skipton Road, Killinghall, Harrogate • 01423 500 340

Old Bell Tavern

6 Royal Parade, Harrogate • 01423 507 930

Offering a diverse choice of real ales and European lagers, alongside good quality pub food in the bar or equally popular first floor restaurant, the Old Bell Tavern is one of Harrogate's biggest success stories of the past few years. With the feel of a favourite haunt it comes as no surprise to find that it is located on the site of the 19th-century Bell Tavern. So good that Bill Clinton decided to drop by for lunch and a pint when he visited the town.

O'Neills Irish Bar

3 Crescent Road, Harrogate • 01423 725 561

Pine Marten

Otley Road, Beckwith Knowle, Beckwithshaw, Harrogate • 01423 533 091

Located on the crest of Harlow Hill, which commands impressive views of Harrogate and North Yorkshire, The Pine Marten is a residential pub set in a spectacular 19th century house and gardens. The gardens are a great place to sit and wile away the hours. Replete with ornamental hedges, and fishponds, this is not your average beer garden. The menu is quality pub food with daily specials.

Rat and Parrot

Pitcher & Piano

5-6 John Street, Harrogate • 01423 565 628 • Open Mon-Sun 11am-11pm.

Fun-size branch of the ubiquitous chain bar with all the pine flooring, outdoor seats and comfy sofas you can eat. Also decent daytime grub and the eponymous grand piano (although no sign of anything resembling a pitcher).

Planet Vodka Bar

2 Parliament Terrace, Harrogate • 01423 505 588

Prince of Wales Hotel

High Street, Starbeck, Harrogate • 01423 884 235

Rat and Parrot

11 Prospect Place, Harrogate • 01423 564976

Located on the Strayside, the Rat & Parrot these days offers few clues to its origins as a Victorian hotel. A one-room venue, modern, bright and airy with a fun atmosphere, the Rat is one of the main entertainment hubs in the town centre, with an impressive range of live acts and sporting events on offer, as well as pool and quiz machines for the more cerebral punter.

Royal Oak Inn

Oak Lane, Dacre Banks, Harrogate • 01423 780 200

Star & Garter Inn

Main Street, Kirkby Overblow, Harrogate • 01423 871 625

Station Hotel

Station Road, Birstwith, Harrogate • 01423 770 254

Tap and Spile

Tower Street, Harrogate • 01423 526 785

Aaah ... Harrogate's real ale mecca. Three dark, cosy rooms and a blackboard to rival any for miles around, ranging from the obvious (Black Sheep) to the lethal (Bishops Finger), plus plenty from the Daleside brewery down the road. Also, quiz night on Sundays, folk night on Tuesdays and jam night on Thursdays.

The Harwood

Station Road, Pannal, Harrogate • 01423 872 570

The Henry Peacock

24 High Street, Starbeck, Harrogate • 01423 883 177

The Iron Duke

Cold Bath Road, Harrogate • 01423 526 100

Having struggled with its identity for a number of years, a new name, new décor, and some great food has finally made The

Food and Drink

Iron Duke a must-visit for lovers of the traditional pub. Less manic than the nearby Old Bell Tavern, and with the addition of good live music, this is the best addition to Harrogate's pub scene in some time.

The Kestrel
Wetherby Road, Harrogate • 01423 797 979
Like its counterpart on the opposite extremity of Harrogate, the Pine Marten, the Kestrel is a warm, labyrinthine Olde English Chain Pubbe that's actually very pleasant. It's absolutely massive, but the open log fires and cleverly divided layout ensure cosiness at all times. Comprehensive, if standard, range of drinks and very good traditional pub food.

The Oak Beck
Woodfield Road, Harrogate • 01423 701 872

The Regency
East Parade, Harrogate • 01423 540 110
Decent meat-and-potatoes boozer on the edge of the town centre. Good atmosphere, friendly locals, pool table, beer garden, all the usual. Also pub quiz every Sunday night and occasional live music.

The Rowan Tree
Hookstone Chase, Harrogate • 01423 885 803

The Skipton
Skipton Road, Harrogate • 01423 503 405

The Stone House Inn
Thruscross, Harrogate • 01943 880 325

The Swan
Burn Bridge Road, Burn Bridge, North Yorkshire, Harrogate • 01423 871 031

The Yorkshire Lass
Harrogate Road, Knaresborough • 01423 862962

Thomas Crabtrees
Cambridge Road, Harrogate • 01423 521 512

Tiger Inn
Coneythorpe, Knaresborough • 01423 863 632

Winter Gardens JD Wetherspoon
4 Royal Baths, Harrogate • 01423 877 010
One of the most striking pubs in Harrogate also boasts an impressive outdoor drinking and dining area. As part of the Wetherspoon chain the menu is inexpensive but slightly predictable, but the expanse of heated outdoor seating makes up for this as it has become one of the highlights of the town's recent Royal Baths bar development.

Woodlands Hotel
Gelderd Road, Gildersome, Leeds • 0113 238 1488

Yates's
11 Parliament Street, Harrogate • 01423 502 365
Surely nobody needs to read a review of a Yates to know what it's like? Let's see now... wooden décor, brass fittings, alarmingly patterned carpet, late opening, pub prices, cheesy music. Why it's called a 'Wine Lodge' is anyone's guess, although to be fair the sighting of a decent bottle of plonk here isn't unheard of. Want a place to get hammered *and* nailed, and still have change for the taxi? You got it.

Out & About

Whether your idea of fun involves a peaceful afternoon spent touring an art gallery or three minutes of hair-raising terror on a white knuckle ride, you'll never be stuck for something to do around Harrogate. The town itself offers everything from beautiful gardens to the 'distinctive' charms of its famous spa water: travel further afield and you'll also find dramatic caves, castles steeped in gruesome history and villages so perfect you'll want to move there.

Parklife

Take some time out of the rat race to visit one of these top five parks and gardens

RHS Garden Harlow Carr

This is the most northerly of the RHS gardens and therefore the best place to see what can be grown 'up north'. It covers over 58 acres of land, including a lake, woodland, fruit garden and the wonderful scented garden. This is not just a garden though: there is also a bookshop, museum, garden centre and gift shop to keep you busy. Last, but not least, is the choice of two Betty's Cafes, where you can rest and feast upon tea and cakes.
Crag Lane, Harrogate, 01423 565 418. Open daily (except 25 Dec) Mar-Oct
9.30am-6pm, Nov-Feb 9.30am-4pm. Admission £5.50/£2 NUS/£1.50kids/under-sixes and RHS members free

Killinghall Moor Country Park

This park is a beautiful conservation area packed with native birds and plants. Unlike other parks in the area, there is no formal planting scheme but there are six football pitches and changing rooms. Perfect for Sunday morning football matches or long walks exploring the rugged scenery.
Barberry Close, Harrogate. Admission free

Valley Gardens

Valley Gardens

Plumpton Rocks

When Queen Mary visited Plumpton Rocks she described it as 'Heaven on Earth' and rightly so. Originally laid out by John Carr as the grounds for a country house, the park has over thirty acres of land to explore. There are endless pathways and woodland, a beautiful lake and of course, Plumpton Rocks. It was thought so beautiful in fact that J M W Turner was commissioned to do two paintings of it. Enough said.

Midway between Harrogate and Leeds on A661. Open Mar-Oct Sat-Sun/public hols 11am-6pm. Admission £2/£1 concessions

The Stray

This huge park wraps around the main urban old town and covers over 200 acres. It is a popular site for picnicking, kite-flying and local Sunday morning football matches and it is also the site for the Tewit Well discovered in 1571 by William Slingsby. The Stray is an important place for locals and a group has been set up specifically to safeguard it.

Central Harrogate. Open daily 24 hours. Admission free

Valley Gardens

Alan Titchmarsh recently named Valley Gardens as his favourite public park and understandably so. There are over 17 acres of beautiful gardens and pine forest here, a rhododendron dell and a wonderful dahlia display in late summer. The park houses 36 of Harrogate's 88 mineral wells, along with a boating lake and a crazy pitch and putt.

Cornwall Road, Harrogate, 01423 500 600. Open daily 24 hours. Admission free

MM

The Stray

Visitor Attractions

Anstey Galleries

33 Swan Road, Harrogate • 01423 500 102 • Open Wed-Sat 10am - 5pm. Sun 11am-4pm • Free admission

The Anstey features a collection of notable artists together with a wide range of guest painters and sculptors from across the world. While the subject matter may vary, they are all united in their aim to broaden the boundaries of art.

Art Apartment

The Mill, Green Dragon Yard, off Castlegate, Knaresborough • 01423 867 606

A three-storey selling gallery of art and design for interiors and gardens, including a range of sculptures in the courtyard.

Brimham Rocks

Summerbridge, Harrogate • 01423 780 688

These curious-shaped rock formations are part of a National Trust park and are popular with families wanting to spot the 'Dancing Bear' or 'The Watchdog' whilst having a picnic. Extra fun can be had by scaring your kids with the threat of pushing the (apparently) precariously-balanced rocks over on them.

Courthouse Museum

Minster Road, Ripon, North Yorkshire • 01765 602 133 • Admission £1

Featured as Ashfordly Magistrates Court by Yorkshire Television for scenes in 'Heartbeat', the former Ripon Liberty Courthouse closed as a working courthouse in 1998 and opened as a living museum. Visitors can stand in the dock

Art Apartment

The Gascoigne Gallery

affordable
paintings

Royal Parade, Harrogate HG2 0QA
Tel: 01423 525000
email: info@thegascoignegallery.com

where prisoners were sentenced to transportation to Australia, learn about the Proclamation of Vice and watch an audio visual presentation of the re-enactment of cases heard during its opening week in 1830.

Fountains Abbey

Estate Office, Studley Royal, Ripon • 01765 608 888 • Open Nov-Feb 10am-4pm. Mar-Oct 10am-5pm • Adults £5.50, Children £3.50, Family ticket £15

With extensive grounds and magnificent ruins, it is no wonder that Fountains Abbey attracts more than 300,000 visitors a year. The deer park is also an important area of nature conservation with over 500 red, sika and fallow deer. There are numerous guided tours, family activities and special events taking place all year round along with educational programmes for the kids.

Gascoigne Gallery

Royal Parade, Harrogate • 01423 525 000 • Open Wed-Sun 11am-5pm • Free admission

The Gascoigne promotes contemporary art with a focus on landscapes and has recently exhibited etchings and woodcuts by artists such as Turner, Miro, Chagall and Matisse. This is a popular gallery that allows visitors to view art in an unpretentious atmosphere.

Godfrey & Watt

7 Westminster Arcade, Parliament Street, Harrogate • 01423 525 300 • Open Mon-Sat 10am-5.30pm • Free admission

Godfrey & Watt

Set up in 1985, this gallery exhibits a constantly changing range of ceramics, paintings, jeweller and sculpture. They also operate an interest-free credit scheme where you can buy pieces of art and pay them off over 10 months.

Henshaws Arts & Crafts Centre

50 Bond End, Knaresborough • 01423 541 888 • Open Apr-Dec, Mon-Fri 9am-5pm. Sat-Sun 10am-4pm • Free admission

Excellent selection of weaving, pottery, paper-making, knitting, jewellery, horticulture, woodwork, music and drama and 3-dimensional work (including felting and mosaic).

How Stean Gorge

Lofthouse, Pateley Bridge, North Yorkshire • 01423 755 666 • Open Easter-Sep Wed-Sun 10am-6pm. Oct-Easter Wed-Sun 10am-dusk. Jan Sat-Sun 10am-dusk. • Adults £4, Children £3

Hidden away in Nidderdale is this amazing limestone gorge. Also known as Yorkshire's Little Switzerland, the gorge runs up to 80ft deep and its rare erosion, which has created a surface gorge in a limestone landscape, means it has been made a Site Of Scientific Interest. Those who are feeling a little more intrepid can explore Tom Taylor's cave, the hiding place of the famous highwayman. After all that gallivanting you can cure your hunger pangs in the restaurant with homemade cakes and lunches.

Knaresborough Castle

Castle Yard, Knaresborough • 01423 556188 • Adults £2.50, Children £1.25, OAP £1.50, Family ticket £6.50

In the early 20th century Knaresborough Castle was transformed into a recreation ▶▶

Local Focal
The word on Harrogate from the people who live there

66 I like the calmness of Harrogate, it's a very quiet place. The Stray and Valley Gardens, and I like the accessibility to the Yorkshire Dales. The Drum & Monkey is my favourite restaurant, and there are some good bars here for the younger age group, like Revolution and the Pitcher and Piano."

Natasha, 28, self-employed

Model Villages

However great Harrogate is, sometimes it's good to get away. But there's no need to travel miles when these surrounding places offer the perfect days out

Pateley Bridge

Nestling somewhere towards the bottom of the rolling Nidd Valley, Pateley Bridge is a small but thriving Dales town — or a fairly big village, whichever description you prefer. Either way, it's picturesque and floral, with a steep high street housing quaint tea rooms, craft centres, various small specialist shops and the acclaimed Nidderdale Museum, which is packed with relics and artefacts chronicling the North Yorkshire of years gone by. There's no shortage of accommodation and places to eat, making it the ideal base to explore nearby attractions like the Nidderdale Way, Stump Cross Caverns and Brimham Rocks.

Knaresborough

If you're exploring Harrogate, you really can't miss its historically rich neighbour Knaresborough. Only about 10 minutes down the road but vastly different in character to its posher sibling, Knaresborough is virtually the textbook definition of 'bustling historical market town'. Set in a magnificent picture postcard landscape, it's far smaller than Harrogate but has plenty to offer: a weekly market (on Wednesdays) that dates back to 1310, a castle, the oldest chemist shop in England, historic streets, boating and some magnificently bizarre old buildings — including a house built halfway up a 120-foot rock face. And

Pateley Bridge

Photo: Paul Harris, courtesy of HIC

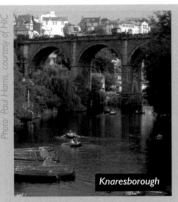

Photo: Paul Harris, courtesy of HIC

Knaresborough

that's without even mentioning the genuinely spooky petrifying well of Mother Shipton's Cave...

Ripley

Best known for its admittedly splendid castle (owned by the Ingilby family since the 15th century, set in a 1,700-acre estate and available for weddings, conferences and corporate functions), Ripley has plenty more besides to offer. The village is rich in historical quirks: its charming mix of stone cottages and cobbled squares, inspired by the villages of Alsace-Lorraine, mostly dates from the 17th century, when it had to be largely rebuilt following the devastation it suffered at the hands of the plague. It's cleaned up a bit since then, but the stocks and weeping cross in the churchyard are a fascinating reminder of muckier times. For sleeping, eating and drinking, the celebrated Boar's Head Hotel is second-to-none.

Darley

'Unspoilt' even by North Yorkshire standards, Darley does boast the Darley Mill Centre, based around a still-working water-powered mill that dates back to 1874. Restored in the 1980s, it's now a retail outlet selling a variety of linens, crafts and clothing. The centre also has a 60-seater licensed restaurant, a children's play area and a mill race. There are also a number of guesthouses and self-catering cottages to hire if you need a base to explore the Dales from, or if you just fancy stopping by for a pint there's the excellent 18th century Wellington Inn.

Spofforth

The most obvious point of note here is the 13th-century castle — or, at any rate, the bits of it that Cromwell's army didn't manage to demolish. Fortunately there are enough of these to be fascinating to those who know where to look, and pleasant for everyone else. Elsewhere? Country pubs, babbling streams, bracing walks along disused railway tracks, weekend cricket and all the fun of the (village) fayre.
MS

© Harrogate International Centre

Ripley

Knaresborough

area for locals, when both a bowling green and tennis courts were created in the grounds. The castle is now Knaresborough's top attraction and the development has continued over the years. The courthouse has now been turned into a museum, which provides an explanation and interpretation of the history of the town and even contains some original Tudor furniture. You can explore the castle independently or join one of the tours that run every half an hour and find out about castle life and hear gruesome stories from the dungeons.

Lightwater Valley

North Stainley, Ripon, North Yorkshire • 0870 458 0060 • Open Mon-Sat 10am-4.30am. • Admission £13.95-£15.50, OAP £7.95

A whole park completely devoted to rides of all shapes and sizes for all ages and sizes. Sound like heaven? Lightwater Valley in Ripon is just that when you have a big family with different tastes to cater for. The park is divided into 'Jaw Droppers' (for big people), Whipper Snappers (for medium people) and Nippers (for little'uns) and each ride comes with particular descriptions of what to expect should Auntie Vera fancy a turn on the Black Widow's Web. There's a slow train to carry the fainthearted round the grounds. Watch out for the 'Valligators', baby Al, Sally and Harry who prance round the park informing, amusing and generally badgering visitors.

March Hare Craft Gallery

1 Ripon Small Shops, Duck Hill, Ripon • 01765 608 833 • Open Mon-Sun 10am-4.30pm. • Free admission

Pumphouse Gallery

Affordable handmade art and craft in a welcoming and friendly atmosphere minutes away from Ripon Cathedral and nestled away in a Victorian style arcade.

Mercer Art Gallery

Swan Road, Harrogate • 01423 556 188 • Open Tue-Sat 10am-5pm. Sun 2pm-5pm • Free admission

There are over 2000 pieces of art on display here, with works from William Powell Firth and Atkinson Grimshaw. The programme of events changes constantly and includes paintings, sculpture and photography. There is often an opportunity to see local artists' work, taken from the permanent display.

Mother Shipton's Caves

Prosperity House, Highbridge, Knaresborough • 01423 864 600 • Open 31 Mar-31 Oct ▶▶

Clear Visions
Elizia Volkmann gets glassed at the Pumphouse Gallery

Snuggling in beside the Royal Pump Room in the Montpellier Quarter, the Pumphouse Gallery is an explosion of light and colour, homing the very best in contemporary glass, ceramics, jewellery design and contemporary fine art.

Proprietor Mark Hinchliffe has been a collector of design and contemporary art since his days working as a chef in central London in the 1980s. There he came into contact with art's avant garde on a first name, have a drink basis and was invited to party with pop's then elite. Short of resorting to major warehousing of his collection, the only choice for him to feed his addiction was to morph into a gallery owner.

For clients seeking great works of design, particularly in glass, Mark Hinchliffe is a guru. What this man doesn't know about 20th- and 21st-century design isn't worth knowing. Since he has turned to fine art, it won't be long before he's the local fine art guru, too. Mark and partner Laura have big plans for Pumphouse; their dream is to bring the world's best designers and artists to Harrogate, in the hope of satisfying the growing tastes of those with cash to splash on beautiful things and incomes to dispose.

1 Crown Place, Harrogate, 01423 520 559

Entertaining the family this summer?

It's child's play with the Kids' Guide!

out NOW!

THE LEEDS GUIDE

Local Focal
The word on Harrogate from the people who live there

❝ I've always known Harrogate quite well. The gardens and the way they keep the flowers is beautiful. If I go out I keep up the top end: if I go drinking I go to the Coach & Horses; if I go eating Chez La Vie or the William & Victoria. There's some great places to eat."

Jamie, 43, building manager

10am-5.30pm. • Adults £5.50, Children £3.75, Family ticket £15.95

Cave and petrifying well where England's most famous prophetess lived during the reign of Henry VIII and Elizabeth I. There is also the Historia museum charting Knaresborough's history,

Newby Hall
Ripon • 01423 322583 • Open 25 Mar-2 Oct. Mar-Jun & Sep Tue-Sun. Bank Hols, Jul-Aug daily. Garden 11am-5.30pm (last entry 5pm). House 12-5pm (last entry 4pm) • Children £5-£6, Adults £6.70-£8.20, OAP £5.70-£7.20, Family ticket £22-£31

Richard and Lucinda Compton, owners of Newby Hall, prove that they have just as exquisite a taste for fine art as they have for horticulture in the gardens and design in the house itself. Much of the work is site specific and will appeal to kids with a love of natural forms and the animal kingdom. Even the more abstract work is so sensitively placed in the gorgeous grounds of this splendid stately home that this makes an exciting and refreshing day out for all the family.

Nidderdale Museum
King Street, Pateley Bridge, Harrogate • 01423 711 225 • Open Easter-Oct 1.30-4.30pm, Aug & bank holiday Mon 10.30am-4.30pm • Adults £2

Situated in the picturesque town of Pateley Bridge and featured on ITV and BBC TV programmes such as the 'Great Antiques Treasure Hunt', the museum has eleven rooms to illustrate the rural life of ordinary local people. There are sections on costumes, transport and agriculture to provide an insight in to lives from the past. There is a selection of tearooms in the village for light refreshments.

Ripley Castle

Royal Pump Room Museum

Prison & Police Museum

St Marygate, Ripon, North Yorkshire • 01765 690 799 • Open Mar-Oct Mon-Sun 10am-6pm. • Adults £3, Children £2.50

Museum tracing the history of law, order and punishment. Housed in the original Ripon prison, the exhibition spans the ground floor and nine prison cells, each one dedicated to different forms of punishment and prison conditions. Children will be able to see medieval stocks, pillories and whipping posts — a good way of persuading them to behave.

Pumphouse Gallery

1 Crown Place, Harrogate • 01423 520 559 • Open Tue-Sat 9.30am-5.30pm. Sun 10am-4pm.

Although small, this long-standing gallery exhibits everything from jewellery to painting and furniture to ceramics.

RHS Garden Harlow Carr

Crag Lane, Harrogate • 01423 565418 • Open Mar-Oct 9.30am-6pm. Nov-Feb 9.30am-4pm. • Students £2, OAP £4.50, Children £1.50, Adults £5.50

This isn't a garden — it's an institution! With 550 acres of gardens to explore, including fruit gardens, wild flower meadow, bird hides and a lake, you won't get bored. You can swot up on your flora at the study centre, library and museum and browse your way through the garden centre and gift shop. And if you are still left wanting more, you can indulge yourself in one of two Betty's cafes. Or both!

Ripley Castle

Ripley, Harrogate • 01423 770 152 • Open Jul-Aug 9am-5am. Sep-Jun Tue, Thu, Sat, Sun 9am-5am. • Children £2-£4, Adults £4-£6.50, OAP £3.50-£4.50

The Ripley Castle has been home to the Ingilby family for over 700 hundred years and through this time they have restored the house and cultivated the grounds. The gardens now house the National Hyacinth Collection and if you visit at the end of April you can see (and smell) these plants in their full glory. There are also tropical plants and cacti and if you take the Park Walk you may be lucky enough to glimpse fallow deer, woodpeckers, rabbits and heron.

Royal Pump Room Museum

Crown Place, Harrogate, North Yorkshire • 01423 556 188 • Open Nov- Mar Mon-Sat 10am-5pm. Sun 2pm-5pm. • Children £1.50, Adults £2.80, OAP £1.80, Family ticket £7

Housed over the famous sulphur wells where for years people came to be 'cured', the museum houses a programme of changing exhibitions telling the story of Harrogate and allows the strong-stomach visitor to sample the strongest sulphur water in Europe — get those fart jokes ready. ▶▶

We're Watching You

The giant golf balls at Menwith Hill are a Harrogate landmark, but who's wielding the clubs?

Set up in 1952 by presidential decree, the American-owned and run Menwith Hill has long been the subject of debate. It is the world's largest electronic monitoring station and is part of a global network of Signals Intelligence bases, which monitor the world's communications.

The 560-acre site is made up of dubious 'official' buildings and the not-so-discreet radomes — gigantic golf balls which cover satellite dishes. The base is said to monitor telephone calls, faxes, computer links and the internet for military, commercial and diplomatic information; however, the American authorities largely refuse to answer questions, give out information or allow reporters, MPs or MEPs on to the base.

In 1997 a European Parliament report made it clear that civil liberties are threatened by the work at Menwith Hill and unsurprisingly, locals have more than a few words to say on the matter. There are numerous action groups, such as Yorkshire CND and the Campaign for the Accountability of American Bases, who are committed to fighting for their liberty and privacy. Yorkshire CND hold regular meetings and demonstrations near the base and at one such event in March 2004, 30 people were arrested. Activists continue to seek accountability and transparency at Menwith Hill but unless the American authorities decide to speak up soon, they could be waiting a long time.

For more information on groups opposing Menwith Hill, visit www.caab.org.uk or www.yorkshirecnd.org.uk

MM

Photos: Yorkshire CND

Mother Shipton's Cave

▶▶ Stump Cross Caverns

Discovered in 1858 by miners looking for lead, Stump Cross Caverns are open to the public with guided tours, video shows, detailed discussions on current academic research to investigate stalagmite drip rates with computerised data.

Greenhow, Pateley Bridge, North Yorkshire • 01756 752 780 • Open Mar-Oct Mon-Sun 10am-6pm. • Adults £4.95, Children £2.75

Uredale Glass

42 Market Place, Masham • 01765 689 780

Set up by Tim and Maureen Simon, visitors to this attraction can observe the glass blowing process and have the opportunity to purchase a piece for themselves. They use a range of techniques, which incorporates functionality as well as design.

Workhouse Museum of Poor Law

Allhallowgate, Ripon, North Yorkshire • 01765 603006 • Open Mar-Oct Mon-Sun 1-4pm. • Adults £1, Children free

Museum displaying the history of Yorkshire's poor, from workhouses to the street, with restored vagrants' wards and Victorian Hard Times Gallery.

Entertainment

Being in the shadow of such a famed party city as Leeds hasn't stopped Harrogate folk from knowing how to have a good time. As well as a thriving nightlife scene — including live music, theatre and clubbing — the area is well served with sports facilities. It's no surprise, then, that so many people come here on short breaks, and we've included a selection of the town's hotels to help you choose somewhere to stay.

HIF The Town!

It's not just lovers of tea-rooms and spa treatments who pay Harrogate a visit — thanks to Harrogate International Festival, everyone from the Bolshoi Opera to Van the Man will be heading your way this summer

Van Morrison

Harrogate's reputation as a centre for arts and culture in the north owes a great deal to the unmissable Harrogate International Festival, which takes place annually, with this year's one from 21 July to 5 August. Celebrating its 40th anniversary this year, the 2005 line-up boasts a varied array of star-studded names from the worlds of music, art and literature, with everyone from classical orchestras to world music superstar Youssou N'Dour heading for the town. The headlining act is no less than Van Morrison, who will be captivating audiences with his musical fusion of R&B, jazz, blues and Celtic folk in a concert on 30 July at Harrogate International Centre which will form the climax of a week of diverse musical and dramatic entertainments.

As openings go, the launch of Harrogate festival is renowned for being particularly spectacular, and this year promises to be no exception. Visitors can feast their eyes on a colorful and innovative collection of street theatre acts — which promise to range from the beautiful to the absurd — in Streets Alive, an event staged in

Youssou N'Dour

the heart of the town on 23 July and catering for the broadest spectrum of ages and tastes.

The festival's finale is posited on equally as grand a scale, albeit a tad more composed than the carnivalesque launch, with the highly acclaimed Royal Liverpool Philharmonic Orchestra playing a trio of Russian masterpieces, including Tchaikovsky's *Symphony No 4*. Conducted by Nikolai Alexeev, of the St Petersburg Philharmonic Orchestra and Bolshoi Opera, and featuring fellow Russian Mikhail Rudy on the piano, this gala concert is a must see for all fans of classical music.

If you cast your eyes beyond the official line up of events and venture into some of Harrogate's numerous galleries, museums and churches, you will also find a variety of independent exhibitions and events. Collectively these form the town's 'fringe festival', capturing many aspects of space and time, from the *Beyond the Caspian Sea Exhibition* at the Mercer Art Gallery to the *Discover Ancient Egypt* display showcased in the Royal Pump Rooms.

This sidelining celebration also includes more family-orientated activities such as organized walks around the town and along the River

Festival Highlights

The Tempest

Those partial to a bit of the bard will enjoy an 'interactive' production of *The Tempest*: expect to be welcomed by Prospero himself, before being taken on a journey through one of Shakespeare's most-loved works. Popular with large family groups, guests may want to bring a picnic along for what promises to be a captivating evenings entertainment.
26-27 July, RHS Garden Harlow Carr

Juan de Marcos' Afro Cuban All-Stars

Co-founder of the highly acclaimed 'Buena Vista Social Club' Juan De Marcos González (pictured) will be bringing northern audiences a little bit of Havana with a performance by the All-Stars. Dubbed as the 'Quincy Jones of Cuba', González has been accredited with raising the profile of Cuban music

throughout the world.
28 July, Harrogate International Centre

Tenebrae, Concert by Candlelight

For those of you seeking something a little more serene, the concert by the internationally renowned Tenebrae choir combines medieval chant with Renaissance works in order to create an ethereal mood of contemplation in the atmospheric setting of St Wilfrid's Church.
3 August, St Wilifrid's Church

Nidd, where amblers can appreciate some of Harrogate's picturesque surrounding countryside. Of particular interest to younger visitors, the Henshaws Arts and Crafts Centre are delivering what promises to be a spine chilling display entitled *When Dinosaurs Ruled the Earth*.

Fans of crime fiction novels would be foolish to miss the Harrogate Crime Fiction Writing Festival, taking place in the town's luxurious Cedar Court Hotel from 21-24 July. To suggest that the event — the only one of its kind — takes a three-dimensional approach to its subject matter is an understatement. Interviews with 'Queen of Crime' Ruth Rendall and US guest of honor writer Michael Connolly are interspersed with talks given by real life experts from the field, who will highlight where the writers stray from accuracy when it comes to describing the more gory

RLPO 's Thelma Handy

aspects of criminal behavior in their novels.

Budding authors of the genre would also be well advised to get their deerstalkers on and attend the industry forum on 'How to get published in the crime world', where industry insiders promise to offer invaluable advice on obtaining a publishing deal. Make sure you get there in time for the announcement of Theakston's Old Peculiar Crime Novel of the Year Award' at the opening night Festival party; where you will be also given the opportunity to mingle with the authors whilst enjoying a pint of Theakston's famous ale.

Tickets are available now by calling the Harrogate International Centre box office on 01423 537 230. 50% discounts are available for the unemployed, under 18's and students in full time education.

HF

RLPO 's Joanna Wesling

Fun, Frolics And Festivals

A selection of the finest events in and about town — and not a glowstick in sight

Junior Drama Festival

This popular festival has been running for 20 years now and its popularity means booking early is a must. The event provides an opportunity for audiences to experience performances from a diverse range of regional young people's groups, who range from four to eight years old. This year, those featured will include North Yorkshire School of Theatre and Granby School in Harrogate. Tickets are on sale now.

6-11 June, Harrogate Theatre. Box office: 01423 502 116

Ladies' Day at Ripon Races

Fancy dressing up to the nines and having a flutter? Then this is the event for you. Make sure you are looking one million dollars (no sportswear, jeans or trainers) as the best-dressed lady wins a champagne lunch for two at the meet of her choice. The event is popular so it's advisable to book in advance.

9 June, Ripon Race Course. Call 01765 602 156 or visit www.ripon-races.co.uk for more details

Nidderdale Festival

For the festival this year, the committee has organised a varied programme that includes drama, folk music from Blazin' Fiddles, talks and exhibitions as well as a wide range of walks and other outdoor activities There are events that will appeal to all people of all ages and interest whether locals or visitors to Nidderdale. Tickets go on sale 10 June.

8-17 July, various venues. For programme call 01423 712 580 or visit www.nidderdalefestival.org.uk

Great Yorkshire Show

This three-day countryside showcase brings you everything from international showjumping to marching bands. This year's highlights include the Great Yorkshire Cheese and Dairy Show and a fashion show. There will also be demonstrations of polo, sheep shearing and fly-fishing.

12-14 July, Great Yorkshire Showground. For show programme ring 01423 541 000 or visit www.yorkshireshow.com

FEVA

Knaresborough's Festival of Entertainment and Visual Arts will be hosting various street theatre and musical events throughout the week. Included in this year's festival will be spoken word performances, an art trail and stalls. The event aims to include everyone and there will be free performances through the week. After taking in all Knaresborough has to offer you can then sample some of the food menus available to tie in with the events!

12-21 August, various venues. For further details visit www.feva.info

Harlow Carr RHS Garden Flower Festival

The theme of the festival will be 'flower arranging through time', referring to the BBC2 series hosted by Diarmuid Gavin in which they examined gardening trends over the last 200 years. There will be flower arrangements throughout the gardens and plenty of chances to swat up on your garden flower knowledge.

27-29 August, Harlow Carr. For more info, call 01423 565 418 or visit www.rhs.org.uk

Contemporary Garden by Diarmuid Gavin at RHS
Garden Harlow Carr

Great Yorkshire Show

Harrogate Autumn Show

Around 90 of the country's leading horticultural nurseries will be in Flower Hall 1, competing for medal award cards and silver trophies and selling from their plant markets. These specialists will be available to share their knowledge and tips with visitors throughout the weekend. There will be a frequent shuttle bus running from the city centre to the show. Pre-booked tickets go on sale 1 June.

16-18 September, Great Yorkshire Showground. Ticket sales: 0870 758 3333

Harlow Carr RHS Garden Apple Festival

This two-day festival will be exhibiting 200 local varieties of apples with opportunities to taste them and get growing tips from professionals. There will also be activities for children such as the family quiz trail. Once you have munched your way through all those apples you can sample the delights of Betty's Cafe and wander round the quaint little gift shop.

22-23 October, Harlow Carr Garden. For more info, call 01423 565 418 or visit www.rhs.org.uk

Farmers' Markets

If you want to find out exactly where your food is coming from, then farmers' markets are the place for you. All products sold are grown, reared, caught, brewed, pickled, baked, smoked or processed by the stallholder, which means you can ask questions and get closer to the sources of local foods. If you're lucky you may even pick up some good recipes to use on the produce you are purchasing.

Monthly, Cambridge Street. For 2005 dates call 01423 556 044

MM

Entertainment

Blues Bar
4 Montpellier Parade, Harrogate • 01423 566 881

A Harrogate institution, the Blues is easily the town's most consistently busy live venue. Veering from mellow to manic, it's invariably packed out through the week. Touring acts, local heroes like Paul Middleton and Jed Thomas, new talent from the excellent monthly Charm night — this little venue has music seeping out of every floorboard and it rocks.

Cardinal Sins Harrogate
11 Station Parade, Harrogate • 01423 701 737

Behind its imposing golden doors, Cardinal Sins has three stylish bars (with tropical fish tanks!) plus a luxurious VIP lounge. Excellent drinks deals and a broad mix of the best in today's music make it the perfect place to celebrate a special occasion, or just to party.

Carringtons
Station Parade, Harrogate • 01423 525 551

One of Harrogate's oldest and best-loved nightclubs, you can really relax and let your hair down at Carringtons, with music to suit all tastes, over two packed floors. Carrington's is also worthy of note for its hosting of the fortnightly Bottom of the Bottle rock/metal/punk night, as well as Pulse 18, a regular evening exclusively for teenagers.

Harrogate International Centre
Kings Road, Harrogate • 01423 500 500

As well as hosting conferences, trade fairs and exhibitions, the International Centre

Local Focal
The word on Harrogate from the people who live there

❝ I came here from Leeds about six months ago and it's been great. Lots of places to go: the clubs still need some work, but Carringtons is always a good night out.❞

Rob, 26, musician

Harrogate International Centre

uses its size to attract some of pop's larger acts, catering for a wide range of musical tastes. This year, look out for Van Morrison, Blondie, The Royal Liverpool Philharmonic and the ever-riffing Status Quo.

Harrogate Theatre

Oxford Street, Harrogate • 01423 502 116
With a varied programme that includes comedy, live music and poetry slams, it's a wonder that Harrogate Theatre find time to host any actual plays. Happily they do, with everything from Pinter to musicals on the bill, not forgetting local am-dram and youth theatre productions.

Jack's

Station Square, Harrogate
Far from its leathery rawk past, Jack's is now leaning more towards the jazz side of things with a regular Tuesday night slot from The

Watermelon Men plus varied guests. *Nnnnnnice.*

Little Wonder Hotel

Ripon Road, Harrogate • 01423 505 352
DIY punk and hardcore gigs in Harrogate? Yes, really. NYHC (that's North Yorkshire Hardcore) to you) are a group of young, tattooed beserkers who put on all manner of loud scary stuff, not just from Yorkshire but all around Britain, and even Europe — mainly in this otherwise fairly sensible pub on Ripon Road. The B&B guests must get a shock...

Odeon Harrogate

East Parade, Harrogate • 0871 224 4007
Harrogate's only cinema is yet to succumb to the fate of many other town-centre picture palaces. So you'll be able to catch all the latest films without having to spend half

Goodlife

**Enjoy the Good Life every Friday
at Revolution from 8pm.**

In the main room join
Sly O'Neil
playing vocal, uplifting funk.

In the bar join
Jim Boroski
playing disco grooves soulful house

Supported by

street couture for men and women

Revolution, Unit 3, Royal Baths, Montpellier Gardens, Harrogate, HG1 2TF
Tel: 01423 858 815   www.revolution-bars.co.uk

Harrogate Theatre

an hour crossing the car park first.

Po Na Na

2 Kings Road, Harrogate • 01423 509 758

Po Na Na is located in the centre of the conference district and frequently hosts DJs and producers of international acclaim, as well as the very best in local talent. Styled like a Moroccan opium den, it is a unique club with winding alleys, comfortable booths and a small but perfectly formed dancefloor. The venue also includes a VIP room with its own sound system and bar.

Revolution Harrogate

Unit 3, Royal Baths, Montpellier Gardens, Harrogate • 01423 858 815

With a range of nights nearly as wide as that of their vodkas, DJs at Revolution play everything from funk and hip-hop to house and disco grooves. Nights include Goodlife on Fridays and Spent on Sundays.

Rat and Parrot

11 Prospect Place, Harrogate • 01423 564976

You know live music's undergoing a renaissance when even the big old Rat & Parrot is getting in on the act. Mainly tribute acts on Thursdays, Fridays and Saturdays, plus acoustic acts on Sunday night.

The Iron Duke

Cold Bath Road, Harrogate • 01423 526 100

The pub once known as the Honest Lawyer has recently been totally transformed with a full refurbishment, but

Rock 'n' Roll Spa

Harrogate may not be up there with Manchester in terms of music legend, but there's plenty of talent around — here's a handful of the best

The Husbands

Based around the intelligent and impassioned songwriting of singer and guitar player Jeremy Grove, The Husbands are a formidable three-piece rock band. Stand out songs like 'Punished' are as strong as anything that the band's heroes Guided By Voices and The Replacements ever recorded.

Xenis Emputae Travelling Band

Phil Legard's one-man industry has produced collection of recordings that are part of the same pastoral psychedelic sound that informs much of Harrogate's most original music. His Travelling Band consists of minidisc recordings that attempt to capture the essential spirit of the British landscape. His sound is minimal, haunting, and truly original.

Tigerbomb

Following considerable local acclaim for his solo album *While The Engines Are Humming Below Us*, Danny Webster's four-piece band are slick, talented, and great live. At their core is a collection of witty, melodic songs that demand to be heard far beyond the leafy perimeters of Harrogate.

Nothing

Like slowly coagulating jam, Nothing improves as time passes. Highly regarded by their peers for their intuitive style of playing and excellent songwriting, Nothing is a true enigma. Singer and guitarist Adam Westerman's demeanour is playful while his band mates remain silent and mysterious with the look of men who know something that you don't.

JL

Tigerbomb

Sound Choices

Tired of the musical mainstream? Give your ears a holiday courtesy of some of these promoters and nights

Hood

Charm

These guys have kept Harrogate supplied with esoteric delights for over seven years (including a period publishing a music magazine of the same name). Currently resident at The Blues Bar, a Charm night will involve the promoters inviting local musicians, artists and writers to bring their own individual tastes to the mix. They've attracted indie luminaries such as Hood and Cinerama to play live, whilst previous specials have included a night of Bob Dylan covers played by 15 different acts.

Pumpleton Sonic Landscaping

Not the latest in 'Ground Force'-style garden faddishness, but a promoting duo who you'll usually find propping up the Stalls Bar in Harrogate Theatre. Imaginative and leftfield, Pumpleton's annual Music Party is an out-there all-dayer, whilst one recent gig called on musicians to play songs based around the theme of storytelling.

The Late Lounge

As the name suggests, you won't find

these folk rushing home after the support act for a pre-bed cocoa. Bar Med's candlelit VIP area and the rare groove and acid jazz tones of resident DJ Johnnie Fredericks provide a fittingly cool hang-out for a selection of live funk, jazz and blues bands.

Jump Around/Bottom of The Bottle
Rock fans are catered for with these two nights at Carrington's. Organiser DJ Trev isn't averse to a bit of themed dressing up; but frequently he's outdone by the live acts, who have included Robochrist, C4 and the chillingly named Liquid Fear.
AB

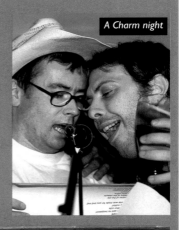

A Charm night

Bar Med, home to The Late Lounge

Revolution

▶▶ it's still the same good-sized music venue it's always been. Leaning mainly towards the covers/jam night side of things, it's always a good place to visit for some good wholesome rockin' entertainment.

Time

14-18 King's Road, Harrogate • 01423 531 896

Recently given a million-pound makeover, the venue formerly known as Jimmy's has something for everyone: Each of the club's four rooms has been indulgently designed with the clubber in mind and surroundings

have been tailor-made to fit in with the different styles of music on offer. For those with an eclectic palate the Connoisseurs' Corner plays only the finest in soul, funk, disco and House. Those who want to schmooze in relaxing and sumptuous surroundings can sample the decadence of the Bacardi Bar, or live it up in the main room to chart, party and pop anthems. The Groove room gives those groovers and movers a chance to get down to some R&B and hip hop flava.

Going out tonight?

Find out what's
happening in
Harrogate, Leeds and York

Get The Leeds Guide

Out fortnightly from your newsagent

Sports Centres and Gyms

Bodyworks Health and Fitness Centre

17 Baines House, Harrogate • 01423 565 330 • Annual membership £28-35 per month, day use £6

The gym jocks of Harrogate are lucky to have Bodyworks. It boasts three gyms in one building, a women-only gym and the largest free weights area in Harrogate.

Harrogate Granby Community Lesiure

Ainsty Road, Harrogate • 01423 502 880

Harrogate Squash and Fitness Centre

Hookstone Wood Road, Harrogate • 01423 536 464

Starbeck Swimming Pool

7 Spa Lane, Harrogate • 01423 883 155 • Gym membership £22-32 per month, squash membership £14.50 per month.

Here you will find four squash courts, a 2000sqft gym, studio classes, sauna, sun beds and a sports shop. Thankfully there's a bar and lounge area to relax in after all that physical exertion.

The Health Club
Central House, Otley Road, Harrogate • 01423 522 177

The Hydro
Jennyfields Drive, Harrogate • 01423 556 767 • Swimming £3.30/£2 concessions. Contact centre for gym prices.

There are three swimming pools, a crèche and a bar at The Hydro. There is also Brimham's Fitness Centre, which has a gym, dance studio and health and beauty centre.

Hotels

Alexandra Court Hotel
8 Alexandra Road, Harrogate • 01423 502 764

Alvera Court Hotel
76 Kings Road, Harrogate • 01423 505 735

Amadeus Hotel
115 Franklin Road, Harrogate • 01423 505 151

Arden House Hotel
69-71 Franklin Road, Harrogate • 01423 509 224

Ashley House Hotel
36-40 Franklin Road, Harrogate • 01423 507 474

Azalea Court Hotel
56-58 Kings Road, Harrogate • 01423 560 424

Balmoral Hotel Harrogate
Franklin Mount, Harrogate • 01423 508 208

Cairn Hotel
Ripon Road, Harrogate • 01423 504 005

Camberley Hotel
52-54 Kings Road, Harrogate • 01423 561 618

Cedar Court Hotel
Queen Building, Park Parade, Off Knaresborough Road, Harrogate • 01423 858 585

Grafton Hotel
1-3 Franklin Mount, Harrogate • 01423 508 491

Grants Hotel
3-13 Swan Road, Harrogate • 01423 560 666

Harrogate Brasserie
28-30 Cheltenham Parade, Harrogate • 01423 505 041 • Open Mon-Sun 6pm-10pm.

Harrogate Moat House
Kings Rd, Harrogate • 01423 849 988

Little Wonder Hotel
Ripon Road, Harrogate • 01423 505 352

Old Swan Hotel
Swan Road, Harrogate • 01423 500 055

Parnas Hotel
98 Franklin Road, Harrogate • 01423 564 493

Scotia House Hotel
66-68 Kings Road, Harrogate • 01423 504 361

Shannon Court Hotel
65 Dragon Avenue, Harrogate • 01423 509 858

Sherwood Hotel
7 Studley Road, Harrogate • 01423 503 033

St George Swallow Hotel
Ripon Road, Harrogate • 01423 561 431

Local Focal
The word on Harrogate from the people who live there

❝ The shops are good for younger people, and older people too I guess. Time's alright for clubbing. It's a good place to go out when I can afford it!"

Sarah, 19, charity shop worker

The Ascot House Hotel
53 Kings Road, Harrogate • 01423 531 005

The Coppice
9 Studley Road, Harrogate • 01423 569 626

The Crown Hotel
Crown Place, Harrogate • 0870 609 6115

The Gables Hotel
2 West Grove Road, Harrogate • 01423 505 625

The Kimberley Hotel
11-19 Kings Road, Harrogate • 01423 505 613

The Kingsway Hotel
36 Kings Road, Harrogate • 01423 562 179

The Majestic Hotel
Ripon Road, Harrogate • 01423 700 300

The Ruskin Hotel
1 Swan Road, Harrogate • 01423 502 045

The Welford Hotel
27 Franklin Road, Leeds • 01423 566 041

The Yorkshire Hotel
Prospect Place, Harrogate • 01423 565 071

Travelodge
The Ginnel, Harrogate • 0870 191 1737

York Arms Hotel
Ramsgill-in-Nidderdale, Pateley Bridge, Harrogate • 01423 755 243

Yorkshire Hotel
Prospect Place, Harrogate • 01423 565 071

Property

From desirable new developments to inspired conversions of historical buildings, there's a property in Harrogate to suit every taste (if not, unfortunately, every pocket). And there are plenty of estate agents around to help you find that dream pad. Happy hunting!

Property Madder

If you're househunting in Harrogate, prepare to have a good long chat with your bank manager first. But, budget aside, the town offers property to suit everyone's taste — or, if you're a footballer, lack of taste

In sharp contrast to the rest of the county, Harrogate's far-from-industrial heritage means you won't find many mill conversions in the town. That aside, there is still a plethora of flat conversions around — many in beautiful, Victorian former family residences. But, with the area's fantastic accessibility to the commerce centres of Leeds and York, prices are some of the highest in the region. So, what do you get for your money?

If you thought you'd never find anywhere in the town centre and still get change from £150K, you'd be wrong. Two-bedroom flats, with views over the Valley Gardens, can be yours for £120,000 to £140,000. The second

bedrooms are often on the small side, but if you're a young working couple - who are the prime buyers of such property - they make an ideal office / study space. All in, a great first-rung on the Harrogate property ladder

Upping the budget slightly, but with the advantage of being slap-bang in the Town Centre, is the new Regent House development. £230,000 will bag you a two-bedroom apartment in this recent conversion. For your money, you'll receive a modern fitted kitchen - with built in appliances included, two decent sized double bedrooms (one with en-suite shower room), plus wood floors and chrome fittings throughout. Properties in this development are

being sold through Hunters.

For those not on a freelance writer's budget, a cool half a million will allow you to almost take your pick of prestigious Harrogate addresses. A number of properties exist within award-winning developments, which can offer Stray views and period features. Interestingly, £600,000 still only buys you a two-bedroom pad with views over Valley Gardens, but you can safely assume the second bedroom is a little bit bigger, you'll get your own parking space, and the bathroom suite isn't an interesting shade of avocado.

For the stock market dabbler, professional footballer, or lucky lotto winner, what does a million and more buy? As you might expect, quite a lot! A pad on the much sought after The Duchy Estate can be yours, or how about the top-floor of a substantial listed mansion house? What the hell, you could even go wild in the country, with a barn conversion in one of the many pretty villages dotted along the Leeds to York rail-line. Then if you've got the money, why not have all three?

That Harrogate can offer property to suit all tastes and pockets, and is a fantastic alternative to city-centre living, the next few years are likely to bring even more interesting and innovative conversions to look forward to.
JT

Estate Agents

Bairstow Eves
15 Princes Street, Harrogate • 01423 529 898

Beadnall Copley
The largest independent in the area has now been established for 13 years — and still run by its founders. Their Harrogate, Wetherby and Ripon branches are all open seven days a week.
8 Albert Street, Harrogate • 01423 503 500

Belvoir Lettings
As property managers, Belvoir will only lend you the house (providing you give them the monthly cheques!) but they do have a wide choice of quality town-centre accommodation.
3 Princes Square, Harrogate • 01423 504 121

Carter Jonas
13-15 Albert Street, Harrogate • 01423 523 423

Dacre Son & Hartley
Dacres are a Yorkshire tradition. Over 20 offices in the County, selling some of the most prestigious property. With period estates on the books retailing at well in excess of £1m, you know you're dealing with one of the big boys. Remember, if you have to ask you can't afford it.
24 Albert Street, Harrogate • 01423 877 200

Crescent Gardens

Davis Estate Agents
5 Raglan Street, Harrogate • 01423 817 799

Hunters
3 Regent House, 13-15 Albert Street, Harrogate • 01423 536 222

Lister Haigh
"I've got a brand new combine harvester". Then the next thing you'll need is some good agricultural land, and no one would be better qualified to sell it you than Lister Haigh. And, of course, the beautiful house in the country to go with it.
5 Princes Street, Harrogate • 01423 730 700

McKenzie Cairns & Hawkins
12 Princes Square, Harrogate • 01423 565 231

© Harrogate International Centre

Myring & Heward
One of Harrogate's newer estate agents, Myring & Heward are attempting to break the mould with their state-of-the-art office and website. As well as an impressive range of property for sale, they also offer rented accommodation. ▸▸

Miraculous Conversions
And now for something completely different ... We reveal what lies in the past of some of Harrogate's best-loved buildings

The Council Offices, Crescent Gardens

The impressive Crescent Gardens building started life in 1871 as the New Victoria Baths, the town's first public bathing establishment. Even then the upper part of the building was host to council meetings, so when the bottom fell out of the bathing business in the 1930s, it was a logical step to remodel the Baths as offices for the Borough Council, which is what they are to this day.

The Royal Baths, Parliament Street

Built at a cost of £120,000 and formally opened in 1897, the Royal Baths were for many years the centre of Harrogate's tourist trade, offering more than a dozen types of bath or douche and a full complement of consulting doctors. The Baths' Islamic arches, glazed brickwork, arabesque painted ▸▸

Photo: Paul Harris, courtesy of HIC

▶▶ *2 Princes Square, Harrogate • 01423 500 777*

Nicholls Tyreman

With the distinction of having their own glossy magazine — *Centro* — focusing on their many new homes and developments,

Nicholls Tyreman proudly claim to be Harrogate's "one stop property shop". And handily placed in Harrogate's "Estate Agent's Quarter" to boot.

9 Albert Street, Harrogate • 01423 503 076

Reeds Rains Harrogate

10-12 Albert Street, Harrogate • 01423 502 274

Strutt & Parker

Established for over 120 years, these are the estate agents for the Premier footballer or lotto winner. Plenty of £1m+ property, and sprawling country estates to be found inside.

13 Princes Square, Harrogate • 01423 561 274

▶▶

The Odeon

Verity Frearson
Tudor House, Albert Street, Harrogate •
01423 562 531

Wigginton Roberts
Don't let the Victorian façade give you the
wrong impression, Wigginton Roberts are
one of the newest independents in town.
Inside bustles with more technology than a
branch of Dixons, and they'll even send
you new property details by text!
9 Princess Square, Harrogate • 01423 568
866

William H Brown
4 Albert Street, Harrogate • 01423 502
282

Your Move
20 Albert Street, Harrogate • 01423 530
700

ceilings and terrazzo floors imported
from Italy all add to its historic fantasy
qualities. Times changed and, with the
exception of the Turkish Baths, all the
bathing facilities had closed by 1969,
precipitating a decades-long decline
that saw the Baths' assembly rooms
being used for little more than coffee
mornings, record fairs and Tourist
Information.

However, from 2002 the building
saw a major scale redevelopment, with
the Turkish Baths expanded and
extensively refurbished. Meanwhile,
other parts of the Baths are now
enjoying a new lease of life as bars and
pubs, all of which manage to maintain
the integrity of the old building.

The Royal Baths

The Odeon, East Parade
When the Harrogate Odeon opened in
1936, it was a cutting-edge piece of Art
Deco architecture. The entertainment
on the first night consisted of a
performance from the Band of HM
16th/5th Lancers followed by a showing
of *Where's Sally* starring Claude Hulbert

Empire Buildings

and Gene Gerrard. Over the past 70 years, little has changed at the Odeon other than the addition of a couple more screens and the lamentable absence these days of military bands — although it's probably less frowned upon these days if you fail to turn up in evening dress.

Empire Buldings, Cheltenham Parade

The place generally known these days as Pinocchios Italian Restaurant has a more chequered history than the smart but unremarkable exterior suggests. It began life in 1872 as a Methodist chapel before becoming the Empire Theatre,

Littlewoods

home of bawdy music hall, circuses and variety, in 1910. The theatre closed in 1931 and was converted to shops soon afterwards but by the 1940s was close to dereliction. Eventually, after some time of being used as storage space for the nearby Harrogate Theatre, in the 1980s the auditorium was repaired to its former splendour and incorporated into the restaurant.

Littlewoods, Cambridge Street

The Scala Super Cinema, opened on Cambridge Street in 1920, marked the arrival in Harrogate of a new concern for luxury and comfort in cinema-building. From then until the end of the 1950s, by which time it was known as the Gaumont, it was Harrogate's largest picture house, overseeing the first golden age of cinema. Sadly, this fine building was demolished in 1962, and the branch of Littlewoods that still stands there today was erected soon afterwards.
MS

Move in
with our readers

Tourist Information

Harrogate TIC
Royal Baths, Crescent Road, Harrogate,
01423 537 300.
Email tic@harrogate.gov.uk
*Open Jan-Mar and Oct-Dec Mon-Fri 9am-
5pm, Sat 9am-4pm. Apr-Sep Mon-Sat
9am-6pm, Sun 10am-1pm.*

Medical

Harrogate District Hospital
Lancaster Park Road, Harrogate, 01423
555 430

Public Transport

Bus and Coach Station
Harrogate & District Travel Ltd, 20A
Station Parade, Harrogate, 01423 566 061

Train Station
Station Parade, Harrogate

Selected Taxis

Central Radio Cabs
18a Kings Road, Harrogate,

01423 505 050
Blue Line Taxis
6 Strawberry Dale, Harrogate, 01423 503
037

Kingsley Private Hire
38 Kingsley Drive, Harrogate, 01423 886
873

Selected Takeaways

Bravos Pizza
2c Knaresborough Road, Harrogate,
01423 880 199

Canton Chinese Take-Away
2 Mayfield Grove, Harrogate, 01423 569
303

Double Luck Takeaway
7 Kirkgate, Ripon, 01765 603 442

Indulge Deli Bar
51 Station Parade, Harrogate, 01423 851
555

© Harrogate International Centre

Harrogate's essential lifestyle monthly

Pick up your
FREE copy now

PLUSH

Harrogate

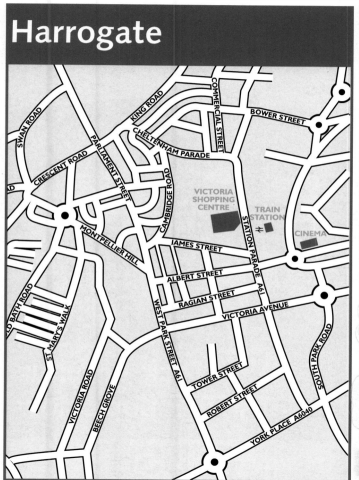

Index

Index